Truth or Dare:
Art & Documentary

Edited by Gail Pearce & Cahal McLaughlin

7. 2008

Truth or Dare:
Art & Documentary

Edited by Gail Pearce & Cahal McLaughlin

intellect Bristol, UK / Chicago, USA

UNIVERSITY OF CHICHESTER

First Published in the UK in 2007 by
Intellect Books, PO Box 862, Bristol BS99 1DE, UK

First published in the USA in 2007 by
Intellect Books, The University of Chicago Press, 1427 E. 60th Street, Chicago,
IL 60637, USA

A catalogue record for this book is available from the British Library.

Cover Design: Gabriel Solomons
Copy Editor: Holly Spradling
Typesetting: Mac Style, Nafferton, E. Yorkshire

ISBN 978-1-84150-175-8

Printed and bound by Gutenberg Press, Malta.

791.
43
TRU

CONTENTS

ACKNOWLEDGEMENTS AND THANKS

We were supported by a number of organizations and people.

We wish to thank the Tate and Whitechapel galleries, WestFocus, Film London, the Arts Council of England and Royal Holloway, University of London.

More particularly we would like to thank the following individuals for their additional support – Heidi Reitmaier and Stuart Comer (Tate), Caro Howell, Don Hurley and Mark Waller (Whitechapel), Michael Uwemedimo (WestFocus), Rose Cupit (Film London) and the staff of the Media Arts department, especially Michelle Rogers for the transcriptions and Jackie Marty and Angela Godden for their administrative support.

We also wish to thank John Ellis for ongoing support, Jane Balfour for contacting Sergei Dvortsevoy in Kazahkstan and Rebeka Cohen for help with editing.

We would like to thank Trinh Minh-ha for permission to use her interview, here published for the first time in English.

We would like to thank all at Intellect for their patience and support.

Finally, we would like to thank all participants in the Truth or Dare conference, who made it such an enjoyable and stimulating event.

Introduction

'Truth or Dare: Art and Documentary' was a conference and a set of screenings that took place during February 2006 at the Whitechapel Art Gallery and Tate Modern. This book is the outcome of that event, combining transcriptions of the talks and conversations, as well as several specially commissioned articles that complement its themes.

We called it 'Truth or Dare' because of the apparent clash between 'authenticity' or 'realism' that documentary has claim to and the association of the imagination and experimentation with art, particularly contemporary art. Our own experience as practitioners and writers encouraged us to question this binary and even the categories themselves.

We noticed how increasingly the boundaries between artists using moving image to explore 'documentary' themes, and documentary makers experimenting with structure, form and content, as well as exhibition possibilities, had brought some film-makers from both disciplines closer together. We also suspected both groups knew little about each other as the two worlds could be hermetic.

The conference was divided into three sections, each opened by a keynote speaker and followed by 'conversations' between practitioners, an attempt to create a discursive and more open platform for discussions. One of the lessons of the conference is that if you encourage the audience to contribute, rarely is the allocated time sufficient to accommodate the demand. It is our hope that these conversations will offer an insight to the practitioners' processes, revealing the motivations and struggles of the creative impulse. This publication, which contains contributions from the floor, will hopefully develop some of the issues raised and act as a spur for further discussions in the emerging common ground between art and documentary.

Our first theme of *Freedoms and Accountabilities* arose from a constant and enduring concern with ethical film-making from the standpoint of documentary makers, and our awareness of how this could change geographically, psychologically and politically, and we were curious to see how these same concerns would be included by artists using documentary form.[1]

In our second theme of *Technologies and Collaboration* we wanted to examine how technologies were affecting the work. Historically, documentary was transformed by the advent of lighter film equipment allowing explorations into increasingly intimate places and farther locations. While noticing how ethnographic and cultural film-making had been affected by this we were keen to include current uses. Artists explore technological innovation as much as film-makers do by using the Web, creating exhibition spaces both in and beyond galleries and working with projection in city streets. Changes in technologies have affected production, exhibition and distribution in both areas.

In the third section, *Spaces and Audiences* are of equal importance to both artists and documentary makers. We wanted to encourage dialogue and the exchange of ideas between them, even while acknowledging that on occasions artist and documentary maker can be one and the same person. Funding, innovation and the search for new audiences seemed to be prime concerns to both artists and documentary makers.

To some extent our choices of categories allowed any speaker to participate in any section as ideas overlapped. Our choices were made more interesting because of this. Clarisse Hahn, with her use of small equipment in private spaces, allowing her to film in hospital geriatric wards, to be an observer at sex worker photo shoots and witness where young men hang out, could have been part of the technology debate. Because of the variety in her ways of showing work, she could also be in the third section. Sergei Dvortsevoy's films, acclaimed in Europe and the UK, have a very different audience in Russia where he is based. He is now considering alternative ways of exhibiting. Ann-Sofi Sidén's experience of recording sex workers at the Czech border (*Warte Mal!* 1999) was exhibited at the Hayward gallery as a series of video booths and projections, allowing the women to tell their stories simultaneously. It could also have been included as part of the Spaces and Audience section. Cahal McLaughlin and Gideon Koppel are both documentary film-makers who have shown their work in galleries. Nina Pope, working with Karen Guthrie as 'somewhere.org.uk', combines live performance with Web exhibition and they are now making films. Jane and Louise Wilson create sophisticated documentary work for the gallery, but would not describe themselves as documentarists. They work with moving image, as does Claudia Spinelli in her work as curator of the Swiss exhibition 'Reprocessing Realities'. The fluidity of definition both in practice and presentation allowed us to offer conversational groups which we thought would be inspiring both for participants and audience.

The keynote speakers were chosen as both links and disruptors to the conference themes. Michael Renov's work on documentary theory has always been radical and influential, and his most recent writing on the film-maker-as-subject seems appropriate to questions of broadening the definition of what counts as documentary. He has noticed and used current debates on art and documentary in the development of his themes.

John Ellis was a fortunate as well as an obvious choice as a keynote speaker. His experience as a producer of documentaries on artists and his writing on the meanings of televisual images and moments offers insight to the mediation of art through documentary, along with their similarities and differences.

Trinh Minh-ha crosses between definitions, not only as a film-maker who makes documentary, drama and art, but also as a writer who has had a profound influence on documentary makers as well as feminists and cultural commentators since her first being invited to show work at, and participate in, the Flaherty seminars in 1983, where she showed *Reassemblage* (1982) 'provoking debate about the assault on traditional aesthetics by a racialised, experimental feminism'.[2] We include an interview with her by Eva Hohenberger published in 2006 in Germany.

We commissioned a chapter from Lina Khatib, who has interviewed Jean Chamoun, a Lebanese film-maker, whose work on documenting atrocities and the pain of war, epitomized by *Tal al-Zaatar*, is included as an example of documentary conceived as art by the maker. The importance of archive and history both to art and to documentary film is also examined.

Gail Pearce has written from the position of an artist and considers how documentary defines itself and whether that changes the nature of her work. From organizing the conference, alternative links and approaches became apparent to her. Including writing by a practitioner allowed us to synthesize the theme of the book and examine the classifications which enabled crossing of boundaries.

Putting together a conference feels similar to curating an exhibition. You choose whose work would be potentially stimulating, you consider the themes, you think about how to group the speakers in order to show them to best advantage. Both the Whitechapel Art Gallery and Tate Modern were enthusiastic and supportive of our ideas. The Whitechapel's remit to provide education and culture for the area in which they are situated was particularly positive for us as artists and documentary makers. We wanted a venue which would foreground the art and give the screened documentaries a, perhaps, new and different context and audience.

Our underlying desire was to ensure that artists who had never considered themselves as documentary makers, and documentary makers who had never identified themselves as artists, could meet and exchange their views of the world. The bonus was that producers, distributors, academics, writers and interested parties could also realize how close these worlds were becoming.

The choices of artists and documentary makers reflected our interests and was further developed from advice by women. Hence, perhaps, the programme was more influenced by issues of gender than race, disability, class, age or sexual preference. Feminism was a thread which ran throughout, but did not dominate, with other issues permeating the programme and discussions.

Gail Pearce and Cahal McLaughlin

Notes

1. For example, see McLaughlin, C. (2006), 'Inside Stories: Memories from The Maze and Long Kesh Prison', *Journal of Media Practice*, 7 (4), pp. 123–133.
2. Sherman, S. (1998), *Documenting Ourselves; Film, Video and Culture, Flaherty's Midwives*, Kentucky: University Press of Kentucky, p. 77.

Away from Copying: The Art of Documentary Practice

Michael Renov

'I think of my films as documentaries. I never fantasize. I have never invented something just for the sake of making an interesting image. I am always struggling to get an equivalent on film to what I actually see'. Stan Brakhage.[1]

The late Stan Brakhage is considered by many to be America's premiere avant-garde film-maker with a career spanning 50 years and more than 100 films. One of his first films, *Wonder Ring* (1955), was a short work commissioned by artist Joseph Cornell who wished to have a filmic memento made of New York's Third Avenue El before its destruction. It is a luminous work, silent, filled with shimmering images that play at the edges of abstraction. Some of these dancing images are reflections captured from the imperfect window glass of the moving car, rippling distortions attracting the eye of the film-maker, neither graphically produced nor optically printed on film. These images are the product of Brakhage's visual fascination, offered up to the viewer as the equivalent of what he sees. It is what we ourselves might have seen had we been there and had we been so attentive.

Critic P. Adams Sitney has called such works as *Wonder Ring* 'lyrical films': 'The lyrical film postulates the filmmaker behind the camera as the first-person protagonist of the film. The images of the film are what he sees, filmed in such a way that we never forget his presence and we know how he is reacting to his vision.'[2] The subject matter of such a film as *Wonder Ring* is the visible world – the stuff of documentary – enlivened by the eye and mind of the film-maker, a dialectical play of subject and object. Although the documentary tradition has tended to repress the emphasis on the subjectivity of the maker in favour of the world on the other side of the lens, the non-fiction film is always the result of an encounter between the two.

Much the same could be said of photography which demonstrated its capacity for the literal transcription of reality as early as 1839. A gesture, a face, an event could now be rescued from time's passage; the photograph delivered an incontestable existential warrant, bearing the physical traces of the light beams that once touched the object itself. The photograph, like its progeny the documentary film, bears witness. But witness to what? To history, no doubt, as long as we trust the image's indexicality, its physical connectedness to the referent, not so easy to do in this digital age. But Roland Barthes for one has argued otherwise. 'I would...say that the photographer bears witness essentially to his own subjectivity, the way in which he establishes himself as a subject faced with an object.'[3] For Barthes, every photograph is a fabulous relic of pastness but it is, even before that, a physical expression of a perceiving self. Subject trumps object.

As a paradigm for documentary film-maker and historical world, I prefer the notion of the encounter, a dialogue between seer and seen, the subjectivity of the maker facing the objecthood of the world. Most often in the documentary tradition, the world rather than the filtering sensibility has taken precedence. But there is nothing inherent to the documentary endeavour that requires that this be so. Perhaps this is the way to describe the simultaneous convergence and disparity between the work of the documentary practitioner and that of the contemporary artist faced with a world overflowing with human drama and contingency. The documentary film-maker has generally opted for emphasizing the social field, the call to arms or public enlightenment, over the lens that filters and focalizes that field. In a literary context, the late-sixteenth-century essayist Michel de Montaigne termed this dialectic between seer and seen 'the measure of sight' versus 'the measure of things.' According to this calculus, the visionary artist opts for interrogating vision itself while the documentarist sets his sights on the world around him and on the need to transform it through his interventions. But I would stress the point that these tendencies have always been emphases along a dynamic continuum rather than defining differences.

That is why I began with reference to the work of a self-proclaimed visionary such as Stan Brakhage or American avant-gardist Peter Hutton who has produced a series of *New York Portraits* which show us a city filled with sky, clouds and changing light conditions. It is a silent city seen through the eyes of a former painter and merchant seaman whose inclination is to look skyward. Hutton produces portraits attuned more to perceptual thresholds and tantalizing visual patterns than to teeming city streets. *New York Portrait, Part III* (1990) is a city symphony cut to the measure of Hutton's visual imagination, presented as a series of vignettes which document the city, the film-maker's sensibility and the capabilities of Kodak's Tri-X film stock which Hutton has used almost exclusively for a quarter of a century.

But why would I choose to begin a discussion of innovations in documentary film-making with references to the work of film-makers outside the documentary canon? In tracing some of the important new directions that have evolved within the realm of documentary film-making in the past two decades, it seems to me crucial to begin by establishing both a conceptual grounding for such innovation as well as a sense of its historical antecedents. I would argue that there has been an explosion of contemporary work in which film- and video makers have explored the historical world from diverse perspectives, employing a range of methods and approaches. These artists are drawn to the world 'out there' as documentarists have since the Lumières but shaped and informed by the world 'in here,' by their personal experience, cultural and sexual identities, their political and aesthetic engagements. There is a new balance being struck between subject and object and the result is a reinvention of documentary practice. In this regard, I will make reference to the uses of personal voice and performance in Marlon Riggs' *Tongues Untied* (1989) and Sadie Benning's *It Wasn't Love* (1992), the combining of live action and animation in Jonathan Hodgson's *Feeling My Way* (1997), the reinscription of documentary temporality in Peter Forgacs' *The Maelstrom* (1997), the revision of the city symphony in Jem Cohen's *Lost Book Found* (1995) and the movement beyond traditional narrative forms in Jay Rosenblatt's *Phantom Limb* (2005). I hope it will become apparent that, while these works are in powerful dialogue with 80 years of documentary film practice, they are also reworking the syntax of documentary film-making and reconfiguring its boundaries. All of which are indications of a remarkable vitality within the realm of contemporary non-fiction media. Moreover these works are bringing the documentary world in ever-closer contact with the realm of contemporary art.

But before moving to the work of the recent past, I would like to return for a moment to earlier strands of formal innovation. Dziga Vertov, one of documentary's totemic ancestors, voiced certain modernist ambitions which constitute, for the documentary tradition, a road not taken. Vertov, pseudonym of Denis Kaufman – newsreel producer, manifesto writer and creator of the landmark film *The Man with a Movie Camera* in 1929 – celebrated the cinema's unparalleled possibilities. In Vertov's view, these possibilities had nothing to do with film-drama, deemed to be 'the opiate of the people'.[4] 'The main and essential thing is,' wrote Vertov, 'the sensory exploration of the world through film. We therefore take as the point of departure the use of the camera as a kino-eye, more perfect than the human eye, for the exploration of the chaos of visual phenomena that fills space.'[5] The camera – freed from the physical limitations of human perception, capable of contracting or expanding time, of plunging and soaring through the heavens, of linking and combining disparate spaces and bodies – could do far more than merely copy the eye. 'Starting today,' wrote Vertov in 1923, 'we are liberating the camera and making it work in the opposite direction – away from copying.'[6]

Here, very early on, a year after Robert Flaherty's *Nanook of the North*, the first documentary blockbuster, Vertov stakes a claim for the entirety of the cinematic apparatus: its mission is to be an infinitely perfectible prosthesis to the human sensorium, a mission inherited by Virtual Reality and other current technologies. For Vertov, there need be no fabrications of drama for cinematic creation; the social world in all its dynamism and complexity provided drama enough. An experimenter with sound recording as early as 1916, Vertov believed that the filmic capture of sound and image and its reorganization through montage could re-present the world in ways that could literally alter the consciousness of its audience. The cineaste's raw material was everywhere around her but to achieve the goal of cinematic creation she could be no mere copyist of nature. She was to transform it through her engagement with it, through much thought, careful selection, framing, composition, sound design and editing. For Vertov, intellection and artistry were the necessary requirements for documentary film-making which was the purest of cinematic modes. One could say that, in the first decade of documentary's emergence, its claims to the status of art by virtue of its unprecedented power to defamiliarize and thus transform the world were aggressively posited.

In my own writing, I have argued for the existence of four fundamental documentary functions or modalities whose interplay constitutes a documentary poetics: the preservational, the persuasive, the analytic and the expressive functions.[7] In my view, the expressive or aesthetic function has tended to be undervalued within the non-fiction domain, a circumstance that has begun to change in recent years. Quite often, the documentarist's task has been to mobilize mass opinion, to draw attention to an injustice or to offer to public view a previously unknown corner of the world. But it is important to note that expressivity is the support of the other discursive goals. The greater the expressive power of the piece, that is, the more vividly the film communicates, the more likely an audience is to feel persuasion, educative value or revelation. The camera that follows John F. Kennedy into that Milwaukee auditorium in *Primary* (1960), the film that, along with Jean Rouch and Edgar Morin's *Chronique d'un Eté* (1961), helped to launch the movement variously called cinema verité or direct cinema, allows us to gauge the man's charismatic power, to witness the laying on of hands as Kennedy winds his way to the stage, in a manner that no other camera placement could have done. The strength of the cinematic gesture heightens the film's power to persuade us of the candidate's extraordinary personal appeal.

The centrality of the expressive domain is a crucial point to make for documentary studies in light of a tradition of disparagement toward 'formalism,' meant to be an unyielding focus on the beautiful rather than the true. Vertov suffered from such an indictment even from comrade Sergei Eisenstein himself who chastised the monumental *The Man with a Movie Camera* as 'formalist jackstraws and unmotivated camera mischief.'* In the 1930s, the Griersonian tradition sought to show the face of industrial Britain to the world, to valorize the state's best efforts and the common courage of its citizenry. During more than a decade of worldwide depression and war, aesthetics tended to be seen as a luxury ill-suited to the urgency of the times.

Perhaps Joris Ivens offers the clearest instance of an anti-aesthetic that emerged within the documentary tradition during the 1930s and 1940s. While filming his monumental *Misery in the Borinage* (1933), Ivens, whose earlier film *Rain* (1929) had celebrated the camera's power to evoke the subtleties of atmosphere and sensory memory, decided that beautiful images could sabotage his goal of alerting the world to the dire conditions faced by striking coalminers in the Borinage region of Belgium.

> During the filming of *Borinage* we sometimes had to destroy a certain unwelcome superficial beauty that would occur when we did not want it. When the clear-cut shadow of the barracks window fell on the dirty rags and dishes of a table the pleasant effect of the shadow actually destroyed the effect of dirtiness we wanted, so we broke the edges of the shadow. Our aim was to prevent agreeable photographic effects distracting the audience from the unpleasant truths we were showing.[8]

Far from moving away from copying as Vertov had wished, documentary makers of the period embraced the documentary cinema's mimetic capacities wholeheartedly as a way to move an audience to grim recognition and social mobilization.

I would nonetheless argue that it is the clickity-clack rhythm of W. H. Auden's narration in Wright and Watt's *Night Mail* (1936) or the flawless editing of people and machines toiling as one to defeat the Germans in Jennings and McAllister's *Listen to Britain* (1942) that burn these films into the world's memory. They do their work to persuade and promote all the better for their ability to engage our senses and induce our pleasures. In *Claiming the Real*, Brian Winston has argued that the Griersonians were more interested in 'prettifying aesthetics' and the search for the picturesque than in investigating the social ills which their films appeared to address.[9] I don't deny the shortcomings of these films' social reformist politics but I must oppose the terms of the critique. The formal construction of a work is far from an add-on or surface feature that the 'prettifying' label would suggest (aesthetics as the icing on the cake). Rather the formal domain is about the work of construction, the play of the signifier, the vehicle of meaning for every instance of human communication. The formal regime is the very portal of sense-making; it determines the viewer's access to the expression of ideas, its power to move and transform an audience.

Thus far I have argued for the centrality of formal or expressive concerns for documentary film-making at both the conceptual and historical levels. I have also suggested that a sort of documentary anti-aesthetic emerged in the 1930s and early 1940s which has marked this cinematic mode ever since. I would argue that it was the dire necessity of that moment that has cut documentary off from its avant-garde roots. Here I'm thinking of the city symphonies of Walter Ruttmann, Jean Vigo and Alberto Cavalcanti, Luis Bunuel's *Las Hurdes* (1932) or later works such as Georges Franju's *Le Sang des Bêtes* (1949) or Alain Resnais's *Nuit ou Brouillard* (1955).

Another institutional circumstance has intervened, cutting documentary culture off from its avant-garde roots. Beginning in the 1960s, television arose as hegemonic across Europe and the United States. The standards of broadcast journalism began to displace those of the documentary tradition in a manner discussed at the 'Truth or Dare: Documentary and Art' conference by John Ellis. What we think we know about documentary has been strenuously conditioned by televisual practices, a circumstance that is now being undone by documentary's new theatrical vitality, a lively festival circuit and the new museum as well as gallery options that are bringing documentary forms (often via multi-channel installations) to new audiences.

Documentary has long borne an asymptotic relationship to commercial culture, uneven and historically contingent. At certain moments – the first of them no doubt coinciding with the tremendous popularity of Robert Flaherty's *Nanook of the North* (1922) – it has seemed that non-fiction forms could compete with their fictional counterparts in the marketplace. In the early 1960s, Robert Drew of Drew Associates believed that his brand of direct cinema could become an American broadcast TV staple. But his independence did not mesh well with network executives who wished to maintain control over their own documentary units. From mid-1961 to the end of 1963, Drew Associates made twelve one-hour films, only two of which were shown on ABC (American Broadcast Company). The remaining ten films were packaged as a series called the 'Living Camera' in the hopes of enticing a network buyer. This never materialized due in part to ABC's decision to produce its own non-fiction programming. A moment of near-convergence (of documentary and commercial culture) never quite materialized.[10]

Until quite recently with such box office successes as Michael Moore's *Fahrenheit 9/11* (2004) and *The March of the Penguins* (Luc Jacquet, 2005) and the massive emergence of reality television – a global phenomenon – in the mid-1990s, the presumption was that documentary could claim little more than its own modest 'market share,' an audience of the curious and the committed. My own sense is that the asymptotic relationship between documentary and commercial culture still obtains; we are simply experiencing a moment of near tangency that could be replaced by a new phase.

The last two decades or so have been a very good time for documentary aesthetics. Innovative instances of documentary practice developing largely outside the documentary mainstream have, through their vibrancy and increasing popularity, begun to reinvent the tradition, leaving it forever transformed. The innovations that have moved non-fiction media 'away from copying' have emerged in quite different contexts by practitioners who may once not have considered themselves documentarists. It is perhaps worth mentioning that many of the contemporary film- and video makers whose works have helped transform documentary culture received their training in art schools around the world in the 1970s and 1980s: Isaac Julien and others of the Black British workshop movement; Peter Forgacs in Hungary; Rea Tajiri (*History and Memory*, 1991) in the U.S.; Canadian Richard Fung (*Sea in the Blood*, 2001); Clarisse Hahn in France (*Hôpital*, 1997); Sandra Kogut (*A Hungarian Passport*, 2001) and Cao Guimaraes (*The Soul of the Bone*, 2003) in Brazil. All of these artists have produced work that has won awards at international documentary festivals. In doing so, they have helped to reconfigure documentary discourse. Moreover, most of the above-named practitioners also produce installation-based works for museums and galleries that extend and make more complex their documentary engagements.

The intent of my intervention is to reclaim aesthetic innovation for the documentary tradition so that the work of these makers and many others like them (Marlon Riggs, Peter Hutton, James Benning, Su Friedrich, Sadie Benning, Pat O'Neill, Jay Rosenblatt and Jonathan Hodgson) makes historical sense when placed within this rubric. Far from being a mere academic exercise, this act of reclamation can expand the horizon of our own self-definitions within the documentary community – makers, distributors, theorists – so that we understand and enact our fields of endeavour quite differently. I would argue that this recalibration of practitioner classification is already well under way.

In 1989 Marlon Riggs produced *Tongues Untied*, a piece that was shockingly different from Riggs' previous work such as *Ethnic Notions* (1986), a solid exposé of racist stereotypes within American popular culture which was nonetheless entirely traditional in format and execution. I will never forget the impact of watching *Tongues Untied* at its premiere at the American Film Institute's Video Festival. From its opening moments in which Riggs literally bares all, voicing an obsessive drive to self-disclosure that can illuminate something of the lives of black, gay, American males once and forever, the tape was vividly compelling. I was left breathless and still am, nearly twenty years later.

In retrospect, *Tongues Untied* looks very much like a turning point in documentary history. It is deeply autobiographical, profoundly performative (Riggs's body and voice stitch the piece together) yet activist and manifesto-like in character. Its final line – 'BLACK MEN LOVING BLACK MEN IS <u>THE</u> REVOLUTIONARY ACT' – reminds us that, as feminist theory, abortion rights struggles and the AIDS crisis had so vividly demonstrated by 1989, sexuality and everyday life are an arena of profound political struggle. But ideas are only part of the package. Riggs's tape *pulsates*. Its polyrhythms are viscerally felt, engaging us even if we resist its politics. What *Tongues Untied* taught us was that documentary could be visceral, sexy, funny, personal and polemical all at once. And the key to its effectiveness was not its gritty realism, its use of rational persuasion but rather its recourse to the stylized, the expressive, the subjective and the evocative.[11] This notion of evocation signals that the maker is less concerned with 'accurate' representation (a notion called into question by the powerful critiques of ethnography since the mid-1980s) and more with outlining the contours of experience, memory or sensation. Films of evocation may create what anthropologist Stephen Tyler has called 'meditative vehicles,' sites of resonance and imagination that may return us to the world of common sense – 'transformed, renewed, and sacralised.'[12]

Tongues Untied defined the terms of a performative documentary style explored in many other quarters. Sadie Benning became an art star when still a teenager. The daughter of film-maker James Benning, growing up lesbian, working class and culturally isolated in Milwaukee, Wisconsin, Benning began making short autobiographical tapes using a Fisher-Price Pixelvision camera given to her by her dad. The early pieces rarely make their way out of Sadie's bedroom. The video apparatus, even one so primitive, marries sound and image. The camera is both a mirror in which the pensive girl inspects herself in brutal close-up and a diaristic machine that records the voiced anxieties and fantasies of a lesbian teenagehood set to the beat of an exquisitely personal soundtrack. By the time of the creation of *It Wasn't Love* (1992), Sadie, age 19, has discovered her vocation as an artist (receiving the fiscal support of Video Data Bank, the archival and distribution arm of the Art Institute of Chicago) and a self-confident sexuality. Benning becomes a prolific explorer of her sexual identity, performing its variation in delicious and hilarious detail, from sultry seductress to cigar-chomping poolroom stud. Like so many other performative documentaries, *It Wasn't Love* appears to collapse subject and object, seer and seen. But like all autobiographical acts, doubt remains as to whether the speaking and the spoken selves can ever be made to coincide. This can be no simple case of mimesis, no copying of one self by another. It is rather the subject's invention of a plastic object-self, staged for the camera, evoking the infinite possibilities of a rebel sexuality.

Jonathan Hodgson's *Feeling My Way* (1997) is a six-minute exercise in documentary boundary-testing. Shot on Hi-8, it appears at first glance to be a cinema verité-style rendering of the London film-maker's daily walk from home to work, a kind of extended POV shot supported by a layered, subjective soundtrack. The piece is far more, however, as the footage has been processed and, at intervals, live-action is replaced by conventional and computer-animated versions of Hodgson's first-person account. The animated sections so fluidly interwoven flicker with life, maintaining shot continuity (in part through a bridging soundtrack bolstered most of all by Hodgson's steady footfalls) while heightening our emotional involvement. Why is this so? In Hodgson's hands, the animated sequences offer a plastic surface on which to register not only the look and sound of city streets but also the film-maker's reactions to all that he encounters. A cat in a window can, in passing, be labelled 'The Family Prisoner'; the sound of a ringing phone provokes a fleeting thought, 'Ring Simon,' that flutters briefly on the screen as a hand-scrawled legend. Here and there, an intercut street map charts Hodgson's precise location – down Richmond Avenue, past the British Museum.

What is most remarkable about the piece is the way that it fluctuates between indexicality – the videographic long take, a sign by virtue of an existential bond between itself and its object[13]

— and utter interiority, something very close to an audio-visual stream of consciousness. These conditions would seem to mimic those of documentary and fiction respectively. But is this in fact so? In *Representing Reality*, Bill Nichols attempted to distinguish between the domains of fiction and non-fiction as a contrast between *likeness* and *replica*. Fictional worlds may bear resemblance to the social world but that resemblance is held to be fundamentally metaphorical. Documentary, on the other hand, 'offers access to a shared, historical construct. Instead of *a* world, we are offered access to *the* world. The world is where, at the extreme, issues of life and death are always at hand. History kills.'[14]

When Hodgson approaches an intersection in live action, we feel the danger of oncoming traffic. As in *The Battle of Chile* (1974–1979), the cameraman *could be* struck down in his tracks. But thanks to the background presence of the verité footage, the animated sections also seem to issue from *the* world but at a metaphorical remove. The horizontal movement of the figure in space is intermittently supplemented by a vertical movement which elaborates on the film's objective progress. As Maya Deren once famously argued in an effort to explain her ideas of poetic cinema, film is capable of retarding the forward movement of narrative to probe the ramifications of the moment via a kind of vertical investigation. If drama adopts a horizontal attack, poetry goes vertical,

> ...so that you have poetry concerned in a sense, not with what is occurring but with what it feels like or what it means. A poem, to my mind, creates visible or auditory forms for something that is invisible, which is the feeling, or the emotion, or the metaphysical content of the movement.[15]

So in this case, the small historical drama of Jonathan Hodgson's daily journey from home to work is punctuated with vertical moments which tell us about the film-maker's thoughts and feelings triggered along the way. I would argue that we remain in *the* world every step of the way, but it is one in which interior and exterior realities intermingle just as they do in everyday life.

The use of animation in *Feeling My Way* allows us to see in an unusually clear way that indexicality, the physical trace of the world left on celluloid, need not be the exclusive grounds for a film's documentary status. One need only think back to Chris Marker's whimsical travelogue *Letter from Siberia* (1957) in which a brief reference to paleontological relics found on the icy plains provokes an extended paean to a gyrating, colourfully animated woolly mammoth. James M. Moran has written about the challenges to documentary discourse presented by pre-photographic history as, for example, the rendering of a dinosaur which, though based on the best scientific evidence, can only simulate an indexical bond to its imagined referent. Of course, many a documentary has been made on pre-photographic topics and that is because, as Moran notes, 'documentary authority never lies *within* the image, but always in the discursive field *around* it.'[16] Thus, National Geographic makes serious documentary films on serious topics, though they may be mixes of science and conjecture. But *Feeling My Way*, like the performative works of Riggs and Benning, shows little concern for documentary authority. Instead it explores cinema's ability to simulate the sensory experiences and psychic processes of everyday life, increasingly the terrain of the new documentary.

The work of Peter Forgacs poses considerable challenges to the documentary tradition as it has evolved in the past forty years. First through the emergence of direct cinema then through the evolution of the interview-based history film (films, in short, of the observational and interactive modes), the analytic and expressive functions of documentary have remained largely underdeveloped. Forgacs' work, indebted to a tendency Peter Wollen long ago identified with the European (as opposed to the North American) avant-garde (Straub, Godard, Kluge), displays both formal innovation and analytic rigor. Forgacs' *The Maelstrom* is a window onto a vanished world, that of the six million European Jews exterminated in the Nazi camps and ghettos. Drawing his images from archival sources and, most tellingly, from the recovered home movie footage of a Dutch Jewish family, the Peerebooms, shot during the 1930s and 1940s, Forgacs shows us a world that is both familiar and strange, private and world-historical.

These rescued images are imbued with uncanny historical resonances through a stunning display of Forgacs' editorial élan. The footage is displayed at varying speeds and with frequent freeze framings that arrest gestures and glances, suspending the inexorability of time. The film's temporality is never naturalistic, 16 to 24 frames per second; the film-maker asserts a control over time denied his subjects. The affectively charged choral and instrumental phrasings of composer Tibor Szemzo impose a shifting tonality. (Szemzo, it should be noted, has been Forgacs' acoustic collaborator for more than 20 years and 30 films.) The superimposition of graphic text or voice-overs explicitly quoting laws, public decrees and political speeches of the period provides a progressive time line and precise historical matrix. There is both an obsessive concern for historicity and a clear disdain for verisimilitude, the sound and surface of reality. We see the amateur footage, bear witness to the everyday rituals of family life and yet it is Forgacs' and our emotional response to what we see and hear that matters most.

For, if Forgacs is a careful historiographer, he is also a dedicated poetician. His work is best situated in relation to a range of allied, time-based art practices developing in Europe since the late 1970s: avant-garde theatre and performance art, minimalist music, experimental film. Until rather recently, Forgacs tended not to identify as a documentarian. But, as I have argued here, the increasing prevalence of formally innovative documentary films, the inclusion of these works at documentary festivals worldwide, and the increasing overlap with the gallery world have begun to alter many such alignments and identifications.

I would argue for Forgacs' work as consistent with documentary's attachment to the explication of social memory. His films document private lives and social milieus drawn from history with unfailing rigour. In *The Maelstrom*, Forgacs has concretized a metaphor of overwhelming natural disaster in which the films' protagonists are embroiled. It is the work of the film to show that these catastrophic events were, on the contrary, wholly man-made. The film opens with grainy footage of massive waves crashing over the breakwater. Simultaneously attracted and repelled by the violence of the surf, a high-spirited throng races in and out of harm's way, testing themselves against the sea. This is the watery version of the oft-cited 'whirlwind of history' into which Dutch Jewry will soon be caught. But it is Forgacs' innovations with the film's temporality which most distinguish his efforts to materialize/concretize the maelstrom metaphor. Through the rigour of his conceptualization and the editing of so many densely layered visual and audio elements, Forgacs creates what he has called 'time swirls.'[17] The fictive Peerebooms are caught up in a vertiginy of temporal overlaps, loopings and juxtapositions just as history had caught up the flesh-and-blood Peerebooms in its coils.

Without question, the documentary film has continued to move outside and beyond the bounds of traditional non-fiction film-making and its narrative strictures. In particular, I'm thinking of a work such as Jay Rosenblatt's *Phantom Limb* (2005), a remarkable piece in which filmic autobiography doubles as a work of mourning. My brief account of it here will do scant service to the film's depth or complexity. Organized in twelve titled chapters that mimic the twelve-step recovery programs endemic to our culture, *Phantom Limb* is film-maker Rosenblatt's meditation on the death of his younger brother four decades earlier and on the guilt and suffering that have haunted family members since. It's a film that takes a terrible and inexpressible family secret as its founding condition and challenge. As a work of mourning, *Phantom Limb* is produced decades after the fact, a clue to the deferred or dislocated temporality that death and mourning can engender. Using text – short, declarative sentences that provide a framework of past events – interspersed with home movies and archival footage, the film navigates a path between personal testimony and clinical description. The twelve chapter headings or steps (separation, collapse, sorrow, denial, confusion, shock, rage, advice, longing, depression, communication, return) narrate a hypothetical process rather than a story form; the extent to which this process reflects the film-maker's own experience of mourning or recovery can only be inferred. *Phantom Limb* offers little by way of resolution or absolution. It is a haunting meditation that, in addition to its aesthetic value, may have some therapeutic power as well. But it also offers a chastening message – that autobiographical films, like all art, can never hope to wholly displace or heal the secrets and traumas they disclose. Yet we remain drawn to these meditative vehicles, perhaps for their purgative powers, perhaps for the mysteries of the heart which they momentarily expose.

But it is the shape and structure of *Phantom Limb* that concerns me here. Unlike so many documentary films from the grand tradition, there is no beginning, middle or end to be discerned here. The film can be likened to serial art in that its succession of chapters, its twelve-step structure, offers a telling that is more cyclical than linear, more incantatory than cathartic. Such a film suggests another way that the path of the documentarist has begun to converge with that of the contemporary visual artist.

I close by adjusting the terms of my argument – for documentary has always been about art – to ask the question, 'What do artists have to gain from documentary culture?' In doing so, I return to the Barthes quotation with which I began: '...the photographer bears witness essentially to his own subjectivity, the way in which he establishes himself as a subject faced with an object.' It is an ethical principle that deserves mention in this context. For in the documentary tradition, the subject is most often faced not with an object but with another subject.

The ethical encounter between film-maker and subject is what is so moving in many works screened and discussed at the 'Truth or Dare: Documentary and Art' conference. In the case of Clarisse Hahn's *Hôpital*, a remarkable bond between maker and subject is evident. Working alone and over a lengthy period of time among elderly patients and their caregivers, Hahn's presence is marked through her occasional verbal exchanges with her subjects, the tactfulness of her reframing (as during an elderly man's sponge bath) and her insistence in bestowing a kind of dignity on her aging and sometimes addled subjects. Gideon Koppel's *a sketchbook for The Library Van*, strings together a series of vignettes of Welsh villagers who respond to the artist's off-camera (and unrecorded) queries in such a manner as to reveal something of their past, their connection to home or a simple eccentricity of taste or temperament. While the library van, shown threading its way through the Welsh countryside, serves as a nominal narrative device, binding the community, *a sketchbook* is really about the stylish revelation of subjectivities – each villager simply yet chicly framed against a stark white backdrop.

These works by contemporary artists, never previously indexed as 'documentarists', bear a family resemblance to current documentary fare. The depth and subtlety of affective and emotional connection between artist and subject mark them as consistent with one important strand of the documentary tradition (e.g., Jean Rouch's deep ties to his African subjects across decades of ethnographic film-making; Barbara Kopple's passionate attachment to the Kentucky coalminers of Harlan County; Julia Reichert's and Jim Klein's empathy for their committed forebears in *Union Maids* and *Seeing Red*).

The expressive function (the least discussed of the four documentary functions) stressed at the outset can thus be said to be supported by what I would now call documentary's fifth function, the ethical function, its attentiveness to the mutuality and commensurability of self and other despite the differences of power, status and access to the means of representation, a 'you' and an 'I' placed in delicate balance. It is the zone of what Emmanuel Levinas has termed 'non-indifference to the Other' arising from the founding obligation self owes other prior to being. Here too – in the realm of ethics – can be discovered traces of the art of documentary practice.

What then *do* artists have to gain from contact or alignment with documentary film culture? 1) Lessons in the transfiguration of historical representation and of sensory experience in the tradition of Vertov, Vigo, Ivens and Brakhage; 2) Support for a more pronounced attention to the social field, a world alive with conflict and challenge, but one that may be transformed through the artist's interventions – in short, social activism; and 3) Insights into the possibilities and risks of ethical engagement with one's subjects, selected others whose place and meaning in the world command our attention.

These are at least some of the stakes of the art and documentary connection out of which is arising a powerful new breed of non-fiction media enlivening festivals, galleries and theatrical spaces around the world.

Notes
* Eisenstein's dismissal occurs in his oft-cited essay, 'The Cinematographic Principle and the Ideogram' in his *Film Form: Essays in Film Theory*, trans. Jay Leyda (New York: Harcourt, Brace & Company, 1949), 43. 'Here we see disintegration of the process of movement, viz., slow-motion. I have heard of only one example of a thorough application of this method, using the technical possibility of the film with a compositionally reasoned plan. It is usually employed with some purely pictorial aim, such as the "submarine kingdom" in *The Thief of Bagdad*, or to represent a dream as in *Zvenigora*. Or, more often, it is used simply for formalist jackstraws and unmotivated camera mischief as in Vertov's *Man with the Movie-Camera*.'

1. Brakhage, S., 'The Independent Filmmaker: Stan Brakhage' in McBride, J., (ed.) *Filmmakers on Filmmaking: The American Film Institute Seminars on Motion Pictures and Television,* (Los Angeles, J. P. Tarcher, Inc., 1983), p. 203.
2. Adams Sitney, P. , *Visionary Film: The American Avant-Garde 1943–1978,* New York, Oxford University Press, 1979, p. 142.
3. Barthes, R., 'On Photography' *The Grain of the Voice,* trans. Linda Coverdale, New York, Hill and Wang, 1985, p. 356.
4. Michelson, A., (ed.) *Kino-Eye: The Writings of Dziga Vertov,* Berkeley, University of California Press, 1984, p. 71.
5. Ibid., pp. 14–15.
6. Ibid., p. 16.
7. Renov, M., 'Toward a Poetics of Documentary' in Renov, M. (ed.) *Theorizing Documentary,* New York, Routledge, 1993, pp. 12–36.
8. Ivens, J., *The Camera and I,* New York, International Publishers, 1969, p. 88.
9. Winston, B., *Claiming the Real: The Griersonian Documentary and Its Legitimations,* London, British Film Institute, 1995, pp. 38–39.
10. See Mamber, S., *Cinema Verité in America: Studies in Uncontrolled Documentary,* Cambridge, MIT Press, 1974, pp. 62–63.
11. For further discussion, see Bill Nichols' important essay, 'Performing Documentary' in Nichols, B., *Blurred Boundaries,* Bloomington, Indiana University Press, 1994, pp. 92–106.
12. Tyler, S. A., 'Post-Modern Ethnography' in Clifford, J., and Marcus, G. E., (ed.) *Writing Culture: The Poetics and Politics of Ethnography,* Berkeley, University of California Press, 1986, p. 124.
13. See Peter Wollen's discussion of the classification of signs in *Signs and Meaning in the Cinema,* Bloomington, Indiana University Press, 1969, pp. 122–123.
14. Nichols, B., *Representing Reality,* Bloomington, Indiana University Press, 1991, p. 109.
15. Deren, M., 'Poetry and the Film: A Symposium' in Adams Sitney, P., (ed.) *Film Culture Reader,* New York, Praeger Publishers, 1970, p. 174.
16. Moran, J. M., 'A Bone of Contention: Documenting the Prehistoric Subject' in Gaines, J. M., and Renov, M., (ed.) *Collecting Visible Evidence,* Minneapolis, University of Minnesota Press, 1999, p. 270.
17. Personal correspondence with the author, 11 July 2000.

FREEDOMS AND ACCOUNTABILITIES

Cahal McLaughlin (interlocutor), Sergei Dvortsevoy, Clarisse Hahn, Ann-Sofi Sidén in conversation

This panel investigated the ways in which freedoms and ethics have been affected in the making of art and documentary. Cahal McLaughlin (interlocutor), has made documentaries about Northern Ireland – the multi-screen *Inside Stories* (2004) – and South Africa – *We Never Give Up* (2002); Sergei Dvortsevoy is a reknowned documentary maker from Russia, whose films include *In The Dark* (2004) and *Bread Day* (1998); Clarisse Hahn is an artist based in France making work about the body and the self, including, *Les Protestants* (2005) and *Karima* (2002); and Ann-Sofi Sidén explores the human psyche in multi-screen *Warte Mal!* (1999).

CMcL
As an interlocutor I wish to contribute to as well as lead the discussion. I will ask the speakers to introduce themselves through their work and I have pleasure in introducing you first to Clarisse Hahn, who is well known in France and whom we hope will become as well known in the UK.

CH
I make my films because I think that I do not have a clear idea of how I have to behave with the 'other' and how to find a common space with the 'other'. So my work questions how we live together and how we manage to live with others. My movies are about individuals and the links they develop with the groups they belong to, like family, religion, work, community etc.

I feel my shooting can only be interesting when I have rid myself of all sense of the exotic or the extraordinary in the everyday life of the people I am shooting. I always choose to focus not on the moment of tension and accentuation, but on everyday common situations. I don't have a voyeuristic relationship to the people I am filming, I like to develop an intimate relationship with them, to be among them. I follow them for a minimum of one year, filming, interviewing and becoming part of their daily life. It is really important for me to allow myself the time to change with them and also to give them the time to express their world and even their contradictions and their doubts.

Les Protestants Grandmère

In *Les Protestants*, my latest movie, the subject is a middle-class Protestant family, my own in fact, a community that is a minority in France. I explored the relationships between the various people and the solutions they find for living together. This film is about how a group of people identifies with each other, it is about a common identity. So I interviewed men, women, children and the elderly about the values they adhere to. I showed how their way of life is organized and then handed down from one generation to the next, from a sense of religious bonding and membership, and from different ways of getting together. It's long, like most of my movies.

In the documentary *Karima*, the subject is a young woman of Algerian descent whom I filmed for a year, and I show her in the intimacy of her family, with her friends and during domination sessions. Karima is a dominatrix, but her practice is only one of the elements of her life. She does not have a particularly original life, she just experiments in a more radical way with the submission/domination relationship that we develop every day in our work, love or sexual relationships. But in her practice, this is a game she is playing, where the actors decide the role they want to take. I was interested in the S&M world because there you can meet people for whom it is easier to speak about their emotions and their sensations. They don't consider the body as something that you have to keep secret.

Karima

The third film I will talk about is *Ovidie*, named after a porn actress I met in the winter of 2000, and we started working together and became friends. For a year I accompanied her on film sets and live shows. I do not show pornography in its usual media guise, rather it is as a reality which enables us to reflect on the relationships established between people. For a few months, I shared my flat with Ovidie and her husband. They allowed me to film their discussions and arguments, then she became very famous in France and later refused to allow me to show the intimate things I had filmed. So that movie was never shown, but she lets me show what I filmed on the porno set, because she doesn't think that this reveals her intimacies.

You can see bodies at work, committed to the fashioning of an image of pleasure. The porn director is manipulating bodies, an edifice of flesh. This film questions the various ways of relating to others – touching, speaking. Where is the point of contact situated, what does it mean to touch somebody? In *Hôpital*, my movie about a geriatric ward in a hospital, the characters' relationships to their own bodies and to that of others hangs between extreme physical proximity and emotional withdrawal. Contact with another's body is never simple even though habit makes it acceptable, that is why medical contact is ritualized and coded, as is intercourse in the porn world.

The American actress in *Ovidie* jokes with an air of nonchalance as a cucumber is pushed up her anus. The way that the actresses joked and exchanged glances is friendly in this scene,

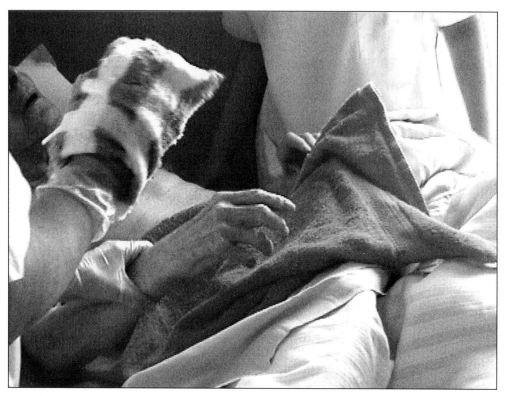

Hôpital

whereas sexual intercourse is professional. Their detached attitude is a form of good manners, aimed at easing the relationship and at making it simpler. I am really interested in the kind of jokes they have in this professional world, which also occurs with *Hôpital*. The black humour of the nurses when they were putting on the track suit of somebody who was paralysed, saying, 'Hey, come on young man, let's go for a little jog' is typical of the humour of the nurses, it's very particular.

CMcL

Thank you, Clarisse. May I now introduce Ann-Sofi Sidén, originally from Sweden, now living in Berlin, and whose *Warte Mal!* was shown to critical acclaim at the Hayward Gallery here in London several years ago.

AS

I travelled to the Czech Republic without really knowing what was going to happen. Originally I had intended to do a work in Amsterdam, in a group show called *Midnight Walkers City Sleepers* about the red light district. They said — 'Here we have everything, you can talk to pimps, you can talk to prostitutes, you can talk to everybody who is involved in the business here'. I walked through the red light district and I felt, 'Oh my God, what a drama', but at the back of my head I had another image. Just after the Berlin Wall came down, a film-maker friend was travelling through the Czech/German border and he saw, as he described it, all these colourful girls in the middle

Warte Mal!

of a dilapidated nowhere. In the dark forest, two worlds met. One part of Europe which is just coming out of a war is trying to make up to the West. And to do that the men put their women out on the streets. So I told the people in Amsterdam that I had another place in mind, and asked them for some money to buy a camera and to make contact with a translator for me. This theme is something that has been taken up before, for instance, the very good Fassbinder movie, *Lola*.

I lived in America from 1993 and I studied for two years in Berlin before the Wall came down, so I had an urge to know what was going on in Europe after the velvet revolution, because, as you know the American media can be quite limited.

I had no idea of how I aesthetically would present the work. As it turned out *Warte Mal!* became a 'village' and each person is a very important member of it. They talk about the same thing but from different perspectives depending on their age, their sex, where they are in their life at that very moment. You get a different slant on the story if you interview a girl who is on her way to work the street or if you interview someone who quit the job a year ago. The work has a kaleidoscopic effect on the viewer. What is not said in one interview is made transparent in another. So I discovered a lot of things about documentary film-making and also about the sex scene. I think for me, *Warte Mal!* does not only talk about prostitution, it's also about men and women. I had nine interviews that were straightforwardly cut, with head shots, not too much scenery or anything. I chose to use the E 55 road, an extended red light district, as structure for the whole installation, so as a visitor you travelled along this road like I did, you could go to the party in the bar, or you could choose to separately go into one of the girl's rooms and listen to their testimonies, listen to the police or a client, or just watch projections of women, pimps and clients along the roads.

Warte Mal!

I kept the editing of the jumpcut heads very dry — most of the time you did not see the interviewee's bodies. The viewer is however very much part of the installation in that s/he is seen choosing the room s/he wishes to enter, like a client. We talk here about how to do things, but I think in the end it's all about storytelling. The same stories are told in multiple voices.

I wanted people to spend time and so I used the museum as a place to exhibit the stories. I have been asked to show this in a single-screen documentary format. I could do it, it would take some work to edit the thirteen hours down to a single screen, but it would be very confining and the work needs to be experienced as a physical installation.

I think that a good story transcends politics and morality. I was criticized in Vienna for not being political enough with *Warte Mal!* and for not giving more of a propaganda speech, but I was overwhelmed with what I saw and heard in the Czech Republic, it was not black and white but different shades of grey. But on the other hand, it is a kind of atrocity that is played out between the East and the West. The truth is that a whole generation of Eastern women had to pay for it. It was the men who sent them out there, or the corrupt system, or whatever you want to call it, who accepted trafficking. The system was collapsing and no one could handle this new situation. Actually the authorities in the Czech Republic let it happen and the West also let it happen en masse.

CMcL

Thank you, Ann-Sofi. Next, we have Sergei Dvortsevoy who is well known in his native Russia and whose work has been screened on UK television.

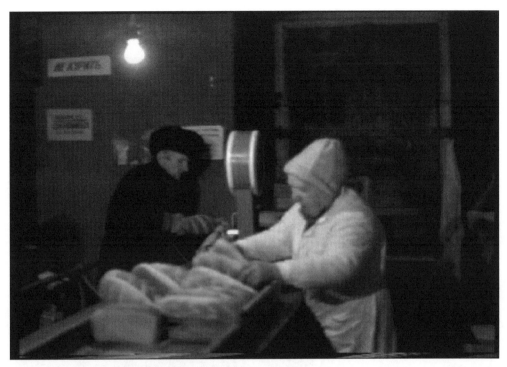

Bread Day In the Bread Shop

SD

I accepted the invitation to come here, because it is very rare that I can participate in such a discussion about art and documentary, or how they are related. I wish to talk about my films *In the Dark* and *Bread Day*, but there are some questions that I want to ask first. What is this 'documentary'? Is it art or something else? I think first of all we have to understand what documentary is. I live in Russia and people there consider too many things as documentaries. For example, some films on Discovery Channel about geography, about science, some experimental films, some fiction and animation, and many television programmes, are all regarded as documentary. I think that this is confusing. Even intelligent people often talk about the 'boring documentary'. Sometimes it is not boring, but I think what I make is art documentary, and if I make art documentary it is definitely art, no question, and maybe absurd art. Can you imagine a theme, about tragedy, about the soul, or about the spirit? As a director I make art of this and I present it to people, I show real blood, real things, real tragedy. I show people and wait for success. This is very absurd. I think we who are making these films are a little bit ill, mentally.

People like to watch this and it can be very beautiful, which is why I make these films, but it is also absurd. The more I work in this genre, the more I feel like a little devil. I can do everything, I can make a lot of different films about one subject, about one situation and the more I work the more I feel uncomfortable, because there is very strong moral barrier that I have to overcome every time and it is difficult for me. That is why I am now making a fiction film.

Desi Waterworth

Billy Hutchinson

Gerry Kelly

Inside Stories: Memories from the Maze and Long Kesh Prison

Another reason concerns the coverage of so-called documentaries which leaves less possibility for making art documentaries. It is harder to find money for an art documentary than it was five or ten years ago. Now more people come from the TV business to documentary and they decide how much time you need to make a film, usually one or two weeks, and they ask, for example, about the blind man who starred in *In the Dark*, 'Why do you need so much time to research?' This is now standard. Our commissioner said, 'You only need two weeks'. How do you know? I think that every subject has its own energy, its own character and special approach. Then there is the issue of its duration. Why do I have to make two-minute breaks every fifteen minutes for TV? Every subject has its own energy and I might want to keep on it for thirty minutes, or an hour or more. TV pressure is very strong, I'm not complaining, since this is reality. So for me documentary is definitely art, but a very absurd and a very difficult art, without doubt.

CH
Why absurd?

SD
It's like a surgeon who cuts a body open and then shows people, 'This is art'. We are doing this with the soul, with the spirit of people and we cut and show the soul, and this is seen as art.

CH
And your own soul too, you are working with your own soul.

SD
If you are making a film about yourself, it is different, but if you make a film about a blind man, you show his soul.

CH
No, you are showing the way you are looking at him, so you are talking about yourself. Your movies are very sensitive.

SD
Of course documentary is not true. This is reality through my frame. This is just part of reality. You don't want to show your soul through fictional stories, but when you show real people this is absurd for me. Usually when I start making a film, I explain to people, 'You need to understand that I will show all that will happen with you. Do you agree?', and they say, 'Yes we agree', but they don't understand how deep I can go, how many things I can catch. Although people are now not so naïve, they don't understand that you really are a little devil.

Inside Stories: Memories from the Maze and Long Kesh Prison

CMcL

As we are in confessional mode, I think I need to say a little bit about where I come from because I want to contribute. As a documentary maker I have moved into showing in the gallery. It came about because I was blocked in the edit suite in the same way that Ann-Sofi said she could not edit all that material together. I only had three participants but still could not edit them together. I had brought them – a loyalist, a republican and a prison officer – back to an old prison just outside Belfast and they remembered their times there. The Maze (1971 – 2000) had been a very violent prison mirroring the violent politics of outside. They told their stories in such different ways. When I tried to intercut their stories into a cohesive narrative, the material didn't work together. A cinematographer, Humphry Trevelyan, suggested the idea of editing separately and showing on three screens.

When it was exhibited in a gallery in Belfast the architecture of the installation coincidentally mirrored the prison's organization, because the issue of association and segregation was central to the struggles inside the prison. The authorities wanted the prisoners segregated from society and the political groupings wanted segregation from each other. When it was shown on three separate screens under the same roof, it made sense. That was not a pre-planned decision, but one that emerged out of the work itself and that was where my interest in galleries came from. There is an opportunity now to repeat this type of recording in a women's prison, Armagh gaol, with about thirty participants and that brings up the issue of how to exhibit. One possibility is to create a digital gallery where audiences can access and create their own documentaries with the raw material.

Warte Mal!

To open up the conversation, there seems to be a common thread that you are all addressing, and it might be described as working with subjects who seem to be marginalized or are minorities in one way or other. Given the freedom we have to be 'little devils', as Sergei says, how is that freedom informed by any sense of accountability to the people we work with, the subjects or participants or collaborators?

AS

I think that subjects think that they are the centre of the world. Everybody is where they are in life and, as Sergei said, it is very hard to explain the consequences to them. Maybe they have never been to an art museum, but they get an idea. I had requests like, 'Don't show it on Czech television', if they came from the Czech Republic. I replied that I wouldn't and have said no to television in the Czech Republic, which wanted to show this piece. I have also been approached by galleries and museums in the Czech Republic and I have said, 'No'. I also said 'No' to a request from Poland. To date, *Warte Mal!* is exclusively seen in the West and this is, of course, a complication.

There was a pimp, Petko, who was arrested in Poland. He held auctions with trafficked girls in a rented hotel and he was finally caught. If I were to show this material there, I don't know what might happen and I don't want to be responsible for that. I think it is very hard to communicate to your subjects what you are doing. I didn't even know what I was going to do with the material at the time that I shot it but I promised not to show it on TV. It was not until I was invited to do a solo show in Vienna Secession, I decided to use this material because I had so much and

In the Dark Making string bags

what was I going to do with it? That was when I began to edit the material, if you will, in an architectural way.

CMcL

Clarisse, did you say that there was a piece of work which you didn't show? Do you always have that relationship with your subjects, so that after filming, if they don't want you to show it, you respect that?

CH

I think so, yes, but I also explain at the start that my works are not only about them, but also about me and my way of thinking. So it is them and it is not them and I think they understand that. Yes, Ovidie did not want some of the recording to be shown and I respected that. Karima, who is not a professional dominatrix — she is doing that with her friends — she really liked the movie and I will show it in Paris in a festival and she will come and present it with me. I continue to make the movie about her. She is very young but she has two kids, so I am filming her as a mother as well.

CMcL

It is not just subjects, it is also the end result, because, Sergei, you referred to the commissioning editor who wanted a fifty-minute piece. The difference between Clarisse's work and a television documentary is that for the latter subjects sign a release form, which gives up ownership of the material. How have you negotiated this with the people that you have worked with?

SD

All my characters are my friends, like my family, but the problem is if you want to make really strong work, a piece of art, you need to research, you need to go as deep as possible, and for art there are no borders, but you can't research everything. I, as an artist, want to research everything and I don't want to feel these borders. But on the moral side, there is a very strong border that I cannot overcome. This is dangerous, not only for them, this is dangerous for me, for my soul.

All strong pieces of work, documentary and fictional films, deal with conflict. If you go deep, you meet tragedy almost everywhere and then you have to decide, do I go deeper or do I stop? This is your decision, it doesn't matter what your theme is, or who your subject is. I think this is the strongest contradiction of the documentary problem – on one hand this is art, but on the other hand it cannot be art because of these borders.

AS

I read in the Berliner Zeitung an interview with Stephen Gaghan, who made *Syriana*, the feature drama on oil exploitation. He explained that researching a subject as a scriptwriter was easy, because it opened doors to all kinds of people, also very rich people. The title of this article was something like 'They Take You as a Joke'. If you are a documentary film-maker, however, then you are going to have people's faces on the screen and that is more difficult to get. I know that some of my girls – I'm talking like an author – they lied or rather altered certain details, but mostly about things that were not so important for the overall story but for some reason embarrassing to them. But it also worked the other way around, things that I might have found hard to tell they told straightforwardly and couldn't care less about.

CMcL

The notion of authorship is interesting in terms of being a storyteller of other peoples' stories. I wonder how you negotiate that? Clarisse, you refer to your films being as much about you as your subjects. Who owns this story, who is the author, or how do you share authorship of these stories with your participants? When I worked in the prison, the way that I guaranteed the participation of the three people was to give them co-ownership. There was never a legal document, but there was an understanding and a trust established from the beginning. Always I made it clear that if they felt uncomfortable, they could withdraw at any stage, right up to the exhibition. One did withdraw several days before the exhibition, but was persuaded to come back in again. I saw myself in that particular situation as a co-author with my participants.

CH

When I work with people, we work together. I have my moral barrier and my films are like I am. It is not a problem for me to see on film somebody who is, for example, a pervert, or cruel. When last night I showed my movie *Hôpital*, in which sometimes people were cruel, some of the audience laughed. Why do you need to laugh about something sad or to criticize it? It is part of the world and humanity, isn't it?

SD

People think that you show some truth, but this is not the case. When you see through the lens, you lie immediately, because this is only part of truth. It is a very compartmentalized truth. Documentary art film is not 'reality', but a reality that a director creates. This is creation, even

Inside Stories: Memories from the Maze and Long Kesh Prison

though we call it documentary, because you point your camera and you construct a frame. From this point you lie. This is art, but not truth. Let us say it is a matter of definition.

AS

Talking about this as art, I think it's also interesting to look at the history of art. Here we have a new medium that's invading the museums, which are normally concerned with making selections and showing work that can be called masterpieces. How do you describe a video work that's fleeting? Of course there is film criticism and that is leaking into art criticism. But I also find that a lot of art critics don't have the skills to look at video. There is limited understanding of how editing and rhythm work, of how things are installed and play off each other.

Of course I have these thoughts about authorship. I did not sign any contracts with the girls. In some cases I was offered interviews if I paid. In the end I realized that it would not be good to do that systematically. So I only paid twice. Mostly, it was about hanging out and spending a lot of time there. One girl led me to another. I think some of the people involved felt relieved that someone was interested in them. As I returned to the Czech Republic over a year's time later I let one of the girls watch her own interview, and with a distance she normally doesn't have to her own life, she cried her heart out and it was very painful for me to witness.

CH

You didn't make people sign because sometimes they are afraid when they are asked to put pen to paper, no?

In the Dark Ivan Nikolaevich Skorobogatov and cat

AS

They just told me their first name, which might not even have been their real name.

CMcL

Returning to the theme of truth, I find the difference between single-screen and multi-screen work relevant. The participants in my film were relating memories from a contested history and my concern was how to negotiate that. This was one problem in the edit suite — how to negotiate a narrative through competing material. But the stuff of editing, the dialogue between people and the dialectic between themes, proved inadequate. When it was exhibited on three separate screens, it was no longer one narrative, but three narratives, three different versions of their truth, their reality. Although most people generally are aware of documentary as having an association with truth rather than truth itself, when you exhibit on more than one screen you make that association more transparent.

Jane Balfour (Distributor)

I come from the documentary side and I'm curious as to how, when you talk about three screens in an installation, how it is set up. Are they in different rooms? Are they juxtaposed to each other? Are they playing at the same time? How does the viewer in the exhibition see it? Do they go between one and the other? I've seen the single-screen extracts here and am curious as to how they might otherwise be set up.

AS

Warte Mal! has nine interviews, each displayed on TV monitors inside small booths, all with plexiglas windows. This is where the oral story is told. There are also four large-scale wall

In the Dark Ivan Nikolaevich Skorobogatov

projections, where the material was more 'ambient' or, if you like, more impressionistic. These were a scrolling diary text of mine, interspersed with snapshot photos, a filmed party in a bar, images of prostitutes standing along the roads day and night, winter as well as summer, and a couple clearing out some forested land.

The straightforward interviews play off and juxtapose the projected images. The installation creates a whole that immerses the viewer, who after a while begins to see the relationship and details connecting the different persons, especially those that I interviewed in Dubi, a small village deep in the mountains on the Czech/German border. The architecture became part of the editing in that both guided the viewer as well as let them explore on their own. I wanted it to be like a street as you walk into the exhibition.

CH
And so we are doing the editing by moving into the space and choosing what we view?

AS
Exactly, that's a good point.

CMcL
Clarisse, you showed in London, how did you set up the exhibition?
CH
BOYZONE, for example, is an installation in progress. It is about male bodies in groups or in the situation of showing their bodies. This is a piece I started 1998, and each time I show it

BOYZONE

there is something new in it. Every time I show it, I look at the architecture of the exhibition space and so the screens are shown differently. It is about the body and it is very important that the viewer can stand in front of the image, within his own body, and move and choose what he wants to look at and what appeals to him. This is a lot about the body of the viewer and how he manages his own body. It is also a kind of mirror, a mirror of your own body and how you are relating to the body of others.

Michael Renov

Thank you for a very enlightening conversation. I want to try to pull together some threads and the first question is for Sergei and your discussion about documentary never being able to approach truth because of the selection process. I wonder if you could comment on a moment from *In the Dark*, which I think you could probably say still conforms to your description. There is a sense in watching your film that you have an engagement with your subject, this blind man. Though, of course, what you are showing us is a very selective view of him, nevertheless the moments when you stop recording sound and you enter the frame, even though your partner who is shooting tells you that you shouldn't be doing this, there is a personal truth there that shows the commitment you have to your subject that extends beyond your need to make the work. I think you could also argue that because you leave that in the film, you are still in control and you are still circumscribing and limiting the truth that you are showing. I want you to talk about your ethical engagement with your subject.

SD
When I started making this film, I wanted to make it 'normally', so that you cannot understand where the crew is, or where the camera is. I wanted to make a standard film, where we observe the person. We show his tragedy, his soul and at the same time he is blind, he doesn't understand where we are, or that we can show everything. This is not an honest conversation. I decided to leave in my entering the frame, because it looks very strange when you shoot a blind man and you show him and he doesn't know where you are. I was here and he knew all the time that I was here and that we were shooting. Of course that is part of the truth, I would say. I wanted to reduce absurdity a little bit in *In the Dark*.

Adam Kossoff, artist, film-maker
I think truth in documentary may be a red herring. Truth is not unethical. What happens in documentary centres on the relationship between the film-maker and the film they are making and the people that they are making the film about. As soon as you point the camera at someone or some object, they become 'other', therefore a documentary is that relationship between subject and object. In Jean Rouch's films you can see that he understands that there is a negotiation between the subject and object.

What I have seen here, and I haven't seen *In the Dark*, is documentary as an old-fashioned kind of transparency, something like a window on the world, which doesn't deal with itself as a medium. My question is, if we are editing by moving through space in the gallery, if that's a definition of what the documentary is and what the moving image artwork is in a gallery, I think we are missing something about what the moving image is. The moving image is surely about constructing something from editing, it is about constructing a rhythmic relationship. If the spectator is moving through the space, doing their own editing, then they are engaged with something which is at a basic level, they not engaged with the manifest material that the moving image should be about.

CMcL
I can give an early response in terms of having worked for years on the single screen, creating 'the manifest edit'. When I showed *Inside Stories* in the gallery, what was revealing was that it was giving over to the audience the power to decide what to see, and how to see it. In one way it undermines my role as a director and editor, on the other hand it allows audiences to partake in the editing. It may not be appropriate for all exhibitions, but it is more transparent process.

CH
When I walked through Ann-Sofi's installation I felt as if I was a client, because I went with a friend, and we thought, 'This one was not bad, let's go and listen'. It was like being on a street.

AS
It's like a lot of things that you make choices about, but which you don't think twice about. That's what I wanted to make you aware of.

Dick Fontaine, National Film and Television School
I have a question for those people who have worked on several screens which means they are giving the viewer a chance to make choices. Do you think that changes the contradictions that

Sergei is referring to, i.e. does that somehow remove some of the responsibilities that he obviously feels quite painfully?

CH

I do not understand why there are so many moral problems. I don't find, for example, what you can see on TV is always respectful. Often there is a tendency to show people as ridiculous and exotic. I think your movie was not like this. I wanted to love him (your subject), and I think there is a part of me who is like him and maybe if I have an accident and become blind I will be like him.

SD

I am happy if you feel this way. I have never made these installations, and for me it is interesting because we so far we have not discussed issues like time, or the effect of more than one screen. When you install your film there is a new dimension, not only time inside the film but also other time. This is quite new for me. On most occasions when I participate in discussions about film-making, whether documentary or film, it is rare to hear film language being discussed, for example, time is very specific in film. I think that we are at the beginning of this. Film is a very new art and we are still trying to understand what it is, how to deal with the image. You shoot on video or on film and now we understand that there is a new dimension, installation, which means many new things.

John Ellis

My point is about seduction, about the relationships that you have all described in various ways, relationships with the people whom you are filming and the taking of a special responsibility for that. In television it always felt to me that it was a kind of quick seduction followed by abandonment. What you did was to say that the entire responsibility for the relationship lay with the subject who was being filmed. If they said something to you then that was their responsibility, they wanted it shown and so you took no responsibility for the onward use and dissemination of that material. You in your various ways have talked about uneasiness with that, and Clarisse's agreeing not to show Ovidie, for instance, was to refuse an entire section of the film. Ann-Sofi talked about not allowing even a gallery installation in the Czech Republic in case it was seen by particular kinds of individuals. This is taking the relationship in a very different direction and there are big costs in not being a 'little devil'.

AS

You said before that art is generally close to media. The nature of a museum is that it allows a limited amount of physical visitors. When dealing with video installations, I think, as an artist, you are used to that. I don't feel that I have to go on a mission with my work. Actually, I feel as if I have shown it too many times in some way already.

Michelle Thomas, Arts Council of England

It is interesting to hear artists talk about the way they are using media because of the illusion of truth that's contained in art documentary making, so I am interested in the subtle interventions that come from choice of media. I want to ask Sergei about *In the Dark* and it seems to me that the work had a painterly quality about it, as if you used a box of colour, with certain angles. It might have been a narrative painting to some extent.

Bread Day Pushing the delivery carriage

Bread Day

Elizabeth Cowie, University of Kent

I would like to a comment on the discussion about the gallery space and installation versus cinema screening. The way in which it has been addressed has rolled out of the dilemma between a performance which is audio visual and the encounter with what people are telling us and the choice of listening and watching. Moving through the space is also moving through an auditory space, which brings into play issues of sculpture, including the volume of the space produced to use the sound. The question which is central to documentary is the performances of the participants and the relationship with overhearing and overseeing and how they are being addressed. The issue is one of interactivity, of walking through and/or editing, and of what we are going to hear and see and the relationship of being addressed.

CH

I was thinking of the difference between the multi-screen and cinema spaces and I thought of *In the Dark* where Sergei shows a man trying to give presents to people and nobody wants to take them or even to look at him. So when you make a film where people are 'obliged' to sit in a cinema, you are in a way obliging them to look at a man that they maybe don't want to look at and there is a different relationship when you are in this space. Those women that Ann-Sofi is showing, everybody wants to look, everybody is attracted to them, so having the viewer frame the space is a good option.

Documentary, History and Reality: Reflections on Jean Chamoun's *Tal al-Zaatar*

Lina Khatib

Documentary film has often been looked at as that which communicates the real, not the imagined.[1] John Grierson's seminal definition of documentary is 'the creative treatment of actuality'.[2] If we take Bill Nichols'[3] point of view, he says that documentaries make arguments about the historical world, a world that exists outside imagination. What we see from the three points of view presented above is a focus on the link between documentary film, reality and history. However, what happens when the real is inaccessible? What is actuality?[4] And what is the role of the film-maker in the chronicling of history?

Jean Chamoun is one of Lebanon's best known documentary film-makers. Starting his career in the 1970s after studying theatre at the Lebanese University and film-making in Paris, Chamoun's work has carved itself a place in the public imagination in Lebanon as a voice for the dispossessed and the resistant. Chamoun's film-making career coincided with the length of the civil war in Lebanon that stretched from 1975 till the early 1990s. Throughout this period, Chamoun's documentaries were consumed with documenting the present: the massacres, the militias and the war atrocities. *War Generation – Beirut* (1988), for example, comments on the Lebanese civil war through interviews with three generations living in Beirut, from the militiamen to children imitating street battles in their games. Chamoun continued to document war in later films, after the civil war ended. *Suspended Dreams* (1992) narrates the stories of four different characters, two of whom ex-militiamen, trying to rebuild their lives after the end of the war. *Hostage of Time* (1994) presents a young female doctor who returns to the south of Lebanon to find her village devastated by 50 years of Israeli aggression. *Women Beyond Borders* (2003) focuses on the harrowing experiences as well as hope of female ex-inmates of the Khiam prison that was run by Israel in southern Lebanon until 2000. Chamoun continues to be a prolific film-maker, mostly collaborating with his wife, Mai Masri, a well-known Palestinian film-maker and producer.

This chapter focuses on one of Chamoun's war-time films: *Tal al-Zaatar* (1976). *Tal al-Zaatar* combines battle footage and personal testimonies to narrate the story of the 52–day siege by Christian right-wing militias of the Tal al-Zaatar Palestinian refugee camp in 1976, and the massacre of 2000 Palestinians in the process. *Tal al-Zaatar* has a unique status as a historical monument among Chamoun's films. What link the works of Chamoun are a sense of duty to narrate history as it unfolds, and the urge to tell stories otherwise forgotten. Chamoun's films therefore compel us to re-examine the relationship between the documentary genre, history, memory and reality. In what follows, I will use the work of Jean Chamoun to analyse this complex relationship.

Jean Chamoun was an active member of the Palestinian Cinema Institute (PCI) in the 1970s and the 1980s. The institute was set up in Beirut by the Palestinian Liberation Organisation (PLO) to document its existence in Lebanon as well as the war in the country, and it involved both Palestinian and Lebanese film-makers. Chamoun (2005) talks of how he and other PCI film-makers would often risk their lives to film live battles at the front lines. Chamoun was one of the first people to enter the Sabra and Shatila Palestinian refugee camps after the massacre in 1982. Following the Israeli invasion of Lebanon, the PLO was expelled from the country. Chamoun was there to film the departure. However, with the disappearance of the PLO, the whole archive of the Palestinian Cinema Institute disappeared. The French government had offered to hold the archive, shot on 35mm and 16mm film, in a controlled-temperature basement. But no one could find the archive to hand it over to the French. Some say it was smuggled out of the country; others say it was destroyed in a fire, or that it has been hidden underground. Since then there have been limited attempts at finding the archive, and Palestinian director Azza El-Hassan made a documentary (*Kings and Extras*, 2004) about its loss, where she traced some of the people who were involved in the Palestinian Cinema Institute. However, *Kings and Extras* is frustrating in this context as it is not entirely about the lost archive, but about lost memory, and presents few clues as to where the archive may have ended up, or to what the archive actually contained in terms of material. Jean Chamoun gives a hint by saying that the PCI film-makers 'tried to film most battles and massacres'[5] during the first decade of the war.[5] One of the few remaining films produced by the PCI is Jean Chamoun's collaboration with Mustafa Abu Ali (a Palestinian) and Pino Adriano (an Italian), *Tal al-Zaatar*. The film is an Italian co-production (co-produced by Unitelefilm), but although it is regularly shown at festivals in Italy, it has not been shown in Lebanon since it was made in 1976.

I had heard about the film while researching a book on Lebanese cinema in 2004. I had spotted a VHS copy of the film stored in a worn-out cupboard at Zico House, an alternative arts centre in Beirut. One of the proprietors of Zico House casually mentioned *Tal al-Zaatar*, saying, 'this film is scary. The director seems to just hold the camera and shoot while people are running away from the camp as it is being attacked'. A year and a half later, I decided to write about the film. I contacted Zico House, but they said they no longer dealt with films, and that the contents of the cupboard were distributed among various people. Several phone calls later and after going around in circles, I figured that the best way to find the film would be through Jean Chamoun. But it turned out the only copy he had of the film is dubbed in Italian. He made me a VHS copy anyway, and it turned out to be in black and white for an unknown reason. Neither Chamoun nor I speak any Italian, and Chamoun had not seen the film since 1976. So on a Friday evening in late December 2005, Chamoun and I sat down to watch *Tal al-Zaatar* together, and he tried to comment on what was going on in the film through what he remembered from 1976. It was frustrating for him, almost 30 years later, not to recall some of the stories told by the people interviewed in the film. It was ironic that the film was a rare PCI production that had survived, but that was doomed to be hidden from the memory of all but the Italians.

It turned out that *Tal al-Zaatar* was also the subject of myth. What I had been told at Zico House was not entirely accurate; the film was mostly reliant on oral narration of the 52-day siege of Tal al-Zaatar camp by survivors. Most of the footage of the attack on the camp was shot by news agencies, as Chamoun and his team were not allowed access to the camp during that time (the news agencies could not get inside the camp, so their footage is limited to that of militias shooting at the camp from the outside). However, the film remains a powerful visual reminder of the harrowing events of the summer of 1976. Chamoun was there when the first survivors were brought out of the camp in pick-up trucks functioning as makeshift ambulances. His camera recorded people reunited with loved ones, the walking wounded, men carrying injured relatives on their backs. It recorded the Palestinian fighters as they loaded their guns, and the people fleeing at the Mathaf crossing between east and west Beirut. Knowledge of Italian is not needed when military vehicles of the right-wing militias who attacked the camp, loaded with armed men, appear on the screen. Even when the film presents oral testimonies by those who lived through the siege, the image is dominant. One of the most powerful scenes is when a middle-aged woman, Um-Karroum, narrates an incident she witnessed. Shortly into the narrative, she glances towards her daughter who is sitting on her left, and the girl covers her face with her palms. Then Um-Karroum gestures with her hands as she speaks, imitating stabbing, grabbing and hitting. I could only imagine the savageness of what she was describing. Then her hands go apart in different directions. At this point Jean Chamoun intervened to tell me that Um Karroum was telling the story of a man over 80 years of age whose legs the militias tied to cars that drove off in opposite directions, tearing the man in two.[6]

The importance of *Tal al-Zaatar* is that it remains the only film made about the massacre, an event that came to be overshadowed by other atrocities in the history of conflict in Lebanon. It is made more pertinent by its inclusion of people who were there during the siege, playing various roles. In this sense, the film can be seen as a witness to history. Chamoun exhibits much self-awareness regarding the recording of events through film, and the relationship between documentary film and history. He often stresses the importance of cinema as a historical 'archive',[7] a document to be referred to after the event. He gives three different reasons for the creation of such an archive. First, an archive exists to ascertain the existence of the event. He says,

> imagine you are living in a war and you are surrounded by battles, destruction, massacres, displacement. You have to cover them for humanitarian reasons. Those who try to hide images of the war are accomplices, who perhaps participated in the war. But those who did not participate have the right to know. I therefore think, from a humanitarian and patriotic point of view, that there should be more films made about the war, although it has ended.[8]

Second, the archive preserves what the event may have destroyed: '[During the Lebanese Civil War] there was an attempt at erasing the identity of the county: the destruction of buildings, neighbourhoods, large parts of cities and villages. Those monuments were parts of culture. Who preserved those? The image. Our attempts, the Lebanese and the

Militant in Tal al Zaatar

Palestinians, were modest; we simply tried to film them'.[9] In this way, film can counter the 'attempted destruction of social memory'.[10] In the case of the physical monuments of Beirut that were destroyed during the war, films documenting them prior to their destruction provide spectators with images substituting actual memories, and therefore take part in what Sorlin calls 'metahistory'.[11]

Third, Chamoun believes in an idealistic role for documentary film. Referring to *Tal al Zaatar*, he says,

this film is a historical document from a critical historical period, so that people can see how monstrous human beings can be, and how careless. This is very dangerous. Its results, if forgotten in history, mean that it might be repeated. Memory is important so that people can learn not to repeat such mistakes, especially the younger generation that has not lived through such massacres and experiences. The importance of cinema and writing about history, about the details, is that one should see them again so the mistakes won't be repeated.[12]

Chamoun's position is aligned with the opinion of Rabinowitz, who states that '[d]ocumentary films provide a stability to an ever-changing reality'.[13] 'The documentary then is meant to instruct, through evidence; it poses truth as a moral imperative'.[14] Looking at documentary as a historical moral lesson may be idealistic, however, it points out the role of film as both framing and being shaped by social experience. As Godmilow argues, '[i]f a documentary filmmaker takes up historical materials, it shouldn't be to produce and/or claim to have produced a comprehensive description of the movement of events, but rather to engage the audience, somehow...in a discussion about ideological constructions buried in representations of history'.[15]

The three reasons given by Chamoun converge into one point, that documentary film can take part in the writing of history.[16] As Raphael Samuel argues, '[h]istory has always been a hybrid form of knowledge...Its subject matter is promiscuous'.[17] Samuel argues that history draws on several sources, both public and private. Chamoun recognizes the importance of private sources of history in his reliance on oral testimonies in many of his documentary films. Oral testimonies prevail in Chamoun's films as they are another way in which reality is presented when no other evidence can be obtained. Rabinowitz mentions how Claude Lanzmann insisted that his epic film *Shoah* (1985) 'is 'art' because only art can ask the questions of history and memory his film attempts to answer: What is the place of visual and audio records in an event whose purpose was to erase all evidence of its occurrence? For Lanzmann the fundamental problem is constructing evidence where no documents exist'.[18] Chamoun's stance on this is simple: 'when people tell you painful stories, they are *showing* you the reality, even if you are not actually seeing it'.[19]

Um Karroum and daughter

The process of presenting reality through personal narration carries its own codes, as '[r]emembering reinforces what is known, because to retrieve a memory is actually to create it anew. Thus, remembering strengthens what has been recalled'.[20] However, remembering as a document of reality has been criticized for three main reasons. First is that '[t]he "event" remembered is never whole, never fully represented, never isolated in the past alone but only accessible through...memory'.[21] Second, because personal narratives have 'voices' asserting the 'individuality of the experience' and imposing 'private feelings and responses upon events'.[22] And, finally, because 'oral texts can change their contents over time, even when the performers intend to produce them accurately'.[23] All three criticisms are challenged in Jean Chamoun's work, especially *Tal al-Zaatar*.

Tal al-Zaatar relies on oral testimonies by a variety of people involved in the siege: we hear from children who have lost their relatives, women and the elderly narrating how telephones, electricity and water were cut off, and medical doctors discussing the hardship faced by those who were injured in the absence of medical supplies. We also hear from male and female Palestinian fighters posing with their guns and talking about how the attack started at 8am with tanks entering the camp, how the Syrians helped the Christian right-wing militias, and how there was an imbalance of power between the invaders and the invaded. The fighters speak of how they did not have enough ammunition and had to ration their bullets, shooting one by one. *Tal al-Zaatar* then emphasizes the self as a product of history.[24] Through the testimonies, Chamoun is able to take us inside the subjects; the focus is not on physical evidence, but on interiority.[25] It is a film that exists on the 'micro' level, relying on 'the director's particular ability to get people to construct their personal histories, often anecdotally, in front of the camera'.[26] This does not mean that the film does not represent 'reality'. In referring to his subjects, Chamoun says, 'I leave people to say what they want. I try to find spontaneous people who forget the camera, to a certain extent. They are in charge, not me. I am recording the reality and presenting it from their own perspective. They all speak from the perspective of their own reality'.[27]

Chamoun's last statement brings to attention the tension between history (as an 'official' version of reality) and personal memory. History has often separated personal and official memories: personal memory has been juxtaposed (as a subjective account) with the objective 'reality' of history.[28] At the same time, the assumed separation between the two carries the danger of romanticizing personal memory as superior to the 'dry' official memory.[29] But Chamoun's films do not necessitate a separation between two modes of memory, nor do they romanticize the personal voice as more authentic. Rather, they recognize that personal memory may have different priorities in the recall of history than official memory,[30] but that it is no less valid as a document of reality.

Personal narration allows people who are normally denied the opportunity to participate in the writing of history to draw their own accounts.[31] The role of the film-maker, when he/she records those narratives, becomes that of the voice giver.[32] In the case of *Tal al-Zaatar*, the film represents 'unimagined existence', the poor and the disadvantaged that are otherwise outside of representation.[33] The camera functions as a link between the personal and the public. By bringing together personal memories and transforming them into collective memories, it offers both an insight into the complex world of individual memories and an expression of shared ones.[34]

The interviews in *Tal al-Zaatar* were recorded very close to the time of the siege, and the film therefore fixes the oral narratives in that particular form. However, narratives of war are open to 'periodic reassessment'.[35] At the same time, '[p]eople remember or forget the past according to the needs of the present'.[36] Chamoun recognizes this aspect of personal narration as reality. He says,

> I, as a filmmaker, may one day make something on the memory of the war through the memory of people. I believe in oral history. I'm interested in recording – when people live through difficult experiences – how people see them and express them after time has passed. When people talk passionately and dynamically about the war as it is happening, is different from the vision of the war ten, twenty or thirty years later. Then things would have matured more. In the future, films can be made about the war that are different from the films made during the war.[37]

In this sense, Chamoun recognizes the necessity for reflection. Reflection may change the way a person experiences an event, and, therefore, the reality, but it is their reality nevertheless.

Consequently, Chamoun rejects the notion that documentary film can ever present an 'objective' version of reality:

> I am against objectivity. No person can be objective. This is a hypocritical word that should be banned. Human beings have feelings that they express; they are part of society; they think. Each one of us has a stance; this is social individuality. You are not made of stone or steel. If a filmmaker simply places the criminal and victim in the same light in the name of objectivity, this is dry and mechanical. When someone makes a film, it stems from their own feelings. You are not distorting the reality.[38]

If '[t]he urge to document is the urge to tell the truth',[39] then what is the relationship between the film-maker and reality? As Trinh Minh-Ha observes, 'though the filmmaker's perception may readily be admitted as unavoidably personal, the objectiveness of the reality of what is seen and represented remains unchallenged'.[40] A story that Chamoun has often narrated summarizes his stance on film as a historical document:

> One time we were filming during the siege of Beirut during the Israeli invasion of 1982. An Israeli plane bombed a 7-storey building in Sanayeh with a vacuum bomb. That was the only time during the war when I stood paralysed. When you see the bodies of people protruding from the rubble, their heads exploded...The building was like an accordion, all seven floors compressed into the space of one. One hundred and thirty-seven people, most

of them children, women and the elderly, were in this building. As I stood there, overwhelmed, the cameraman asked me what to do. I thought, if I don't film now, the historical document won't exist and no one would see it.[41]

Chamoun ended up using the footage in a film titled *Under the Rubble*, which he completed in 1983. The film followed Chamoun's urge to record reality in its presentation of live footage of the Israeli invasion of Lebanon. At one point, Chamoun and his cameraman risked their lives by going to the 14th floor of a building to get a closer shot of the Israeli planes as they bombed Beirut.

Why the urge to film, to be there when such events are unravelling? Chamoun's answer is that 'the war was not an ordinary "event". I could not control the situation around me. You could not stop the war. You tried, with the camera, to record the reality'.[42] Chamoun's statement about not being in control – of the war, or of the people giving oral testimonies to his camera – resonates with the definition of documentary films as those 'which give up control of the events being filmed'.[43] But it is also coupled with a sense of duty to record and narrate, an awareness of being a witness to history. This can be related to the 'pressure of events, what we like to think of as history, and which we *expect* to be reflected, constructed, and interpreted for us'.[44] This is perhaps why, in Arabic, there are two words for documentary films, '*watha'iqi*' and '*tasjili*'. But the second term, which can be translated as 'the record film', is fiercely rejected by Chamoun. This is because it implies neglect of the role of the director or even the camera operator.[45] In short, it conceals the act of mediation that occurs when the camera sees something, and the artistic process through which documentary films are made. The other term, '*watha'iqi*', refers to documentary film as a 'document'—open to dramatization and interpretation.

Documentary film is not about pure description.[46] Documentary film can chronicle history, but it goes beyond the gathering of facts:

> The historian's intervention is posterior to the date, which is already constituted; the documentarist intervenes at both moments in the constitution of the historic discourse. He does not simply rework...the material that history presents him, he doesn't only give a discursive form to the 'documents'...Rather, he shapes the material of which the documents are constituted.[47]

When it comes to being there when the 'event' is happening, '[c]ertainly, real-life happenings were being documented on the screen. Just as certainly, they were being dramatised. Point of view, framing of shot, length of take —all constructed the record at the moment of its mere recording'.[48]

Rabinowitz writes: 'Solanas and Getino advocated a cinema which intervened in history. These two poles – activist/interventionist cinema and a cinema of detached observation – appear miles apart, but the subject chosen for observation can actually elicit intervention and the activist filmmaker might find himself an observer to history'.[49] *Tal al-Zaatar* is an example of how documentary film can transcend such categories. It merges observation with activism. Chamoun's role in the film, then, becomes complex. He is at once witness, interventionist, voice giver, interpreter and history writer.

Notes

1. Stott, W., *Documentary Expression and Thirties America*, (Oxford, Oxford University Press, 1973).
2. Grierson, J., 'The First Principles of Documentary', in Hardy, F. (ed.), *Grierson on Documentary*, pp. 145–156, (London, Faber and Faber, 1966), p. 147.
3. Nichols, B., *Representing Reality: Issues and Concepts in Documentary*, (Bloomington, Indiana University Press, 1991).
4. Eitzen, D., 'When is a Documentary?: Documentary as a Mode of Reception', *Cinema Journal*, volume 35, issue 1, autumn 1995, pp. 81–102.
5. Chamoun, J., interview with Lina Khatib, Beirut, 30 December 2005.
6. *Ibid.*
7. Chamoun, J., interview with Hassan Bdeir. *Al Ahd* newspaper, 26 November 1993; Chamoun, J., interview with George Ki'di, *An-Nahar* newspaper, 13 November 2001; *ibid.*
8. Chamoun, J., interview with Lina Khatib.
9. *Ibid.*
10. Merridale, C., 'War, Death, and Remembrance in Soviet Russia', in Winter, J. and Sivan, E. (eds.), *War and Remembrance in the Twentieth Century*, pp. 61–83, (Cambridge, Cambridge University Press, 1999), p. 63.
11. Sorlin, P., 'Children as War Victims in Postwar European Cinema', in Winter, J. and Sivan, E. (eds.), *War and Remembrance in the Twentieth Century*, pp. 104–124. (Cambridge, Cambridge University Press, 1999), p. 107.
12. Chamoun, J., interview with Lina Khatib.
13. Rabinowitz, P., 'Wreckage upon Wreckage: History, Documentary and the Ruins of Memory', *History and Theory*, 32(2): 119–137, May 1993, p. 120.
14. Rabinowitz, P., 'Wreckage upon Wreckage', p. 121.
15. Godmilow, J., 'How Real is the Reality in Documentary Film?' (Interview with Ann-Louise Shapiro), *History and Theory*, volume 36, issue 4, pp. 80–101, December 1997, p. 83.
16. Chamoun, J., interview with George Ki'di.
17. Samuel, R., *Theatres of Memory*. London, Verso, 1994, p. x.
18. Rabinowitz, P., 'Wreckage upon Wreckage', p. 129.
19. Chamoun, J., 'The Arabic Lens', *Al-Jazeera*, Saturday 22 April 2006.
20. Joyce, R. A., 'Concrete Memories: Fragments of the Classic Maya Past (500–1000 AD), in Van Dyke, R. M. and Alcock, S. E. (eds.), *Archaeologies of Memory*, pp. 104–125, (Oxford, Blackwell, 2003), p. 107.
21. Williams, L., 'Mirrors without Memories: Truth, History and the New Documentary', *Film Quarterly*, volume 46, issue 3, pp. 9–21, spring 1993, p. 15.
22. Hynes, S., 'Personal Narratives and Commemoration', in Winter, J. and Sivan, E. (eds.), *War and Remembrance in the Twentieth Century*, pp. 205–220, (Cambridge, Cambridge University Press, 1999), p. 206.
23. Bradley, R., 'The Translation of Time', in Van Dyke, R. M. and Alcock, S. E. (eds.), *Archaeologies of Memory*, pp. 221–227, (Oxford, Blackwell, 2003), p. 222.
24. Harper, S., 'Popular Film, Popular Memory: The Case of the Second World War', in Evans, M. and Lunn, K. (eds.), *War and Memory in the Twentieth Century*, (Oxford, Berg, 1997), pp. 163–176.
25. Nichols, B., 'History, Myth and Narrative in Documentary', *Film Quarterly*, volume 41, issue 1, autumn 1987, pp. 9–20.

26. Jones, S., 'Marcel Ophlüs' *November Days*: The Forming and Performing of Documentary History', in Barta, T. (ed.), *Screening the Past: Film and the Representation of History*, pp. 149–166, (London, Praeger, 1998), p. 158.
27. Chamoun, J., interview with Lina Khatib.
28. Winter, J. and Sivan, E., 'Setting the Framework', in Winter, J. and Sivan, E. (eds.), *War and Remembrance in the Twentieth Century*, (Cambridge, Cambridge University Press, 1999), pp. 6–39.
29. Harper, S., 'Popular Film, Popular Memory'.
30. Samuel, R., *Theatres of Memory*.
31. Harper, S., 'Popular Film, Popular Memory'.
32. See Trinh, M. H., 'Documentary Is/Not a Name', *October*, volume 52, spring 1990, pp. 76–98.
33. Stott, W., *Documentary Expression and Thirties America*, p. 153.
34. Shaw, M., 'Past Wars and Present Conflicts: From the Second World War to the Gulf War', in Evans, M. and Lunn, K. (eds.), *War and Memory in the Twentieth Century*, (Oxford, Berg, 1997), pp. 191–204.
35. Merridale, C., 'War, Death, and Remembrance in Soviet Russia', p. 61.
36. Van Dyke, R. M. and Alcock, S. E., 'Archaeologies of Memory: An Introduction', in Van Dyke, R. M. and Alcock, S. E. (eds.), *Archaeologies of Memory*, pp. 1–13, (Oxford, Blackwell, 2003), p. 3.
37. Chamoun, J., interview with Lina Khatib.
38. *Ibid.*
39. Sklar, R., 'Documentary: Artifice in the Service of Truth', *Reviews in American History*, volume 3, issue 3, pp. 299–304, September 1975, pp. 299–300.
40. Trinh, M. H., 'Documentary Is/Not a Name', p. 83.
41. Chamoun, J., interview with Lina Khatib.
42. Chamoun, J., interview with Lina Khatib.
43. Eitzen, D., 'When is a Documentary?', p. 82.
44. Jones, S., 'Marcel Ophlüs' *November Days*', p. 149, my emphasis.
45. Chamoun, J., interview with Lina Khatib.
46. Godmilow, J., 'How Real is the Reality in Documentary Film?'
47. Guynn, W., *A Cinema of Nonfiction*, (London, Associated University Presses, 1990), p. 17.
48. Barta, T., 'Screening the Past: History Since the Cinema', in Barta, T. (ed.), *Screening the Past: Film and the Representation of History*, pp. 1–18, (London, Praeger, 1998), p. 4.
49. Rabinowitz, P., 'Wreckage upon Wreckage', p. 127.

Dancing to Different Tunes: Ethical Differences in Approaches to Factual Film-making

John Ellis

The original Film Society, founded in 1925 in London, combined scientific documentaries, social documentaries like Grierson's *Drifters* (1929), avant-garde films like *Berlin: Symphony of a City* (Rutman, 1928) and the Soviet films of Eisenstein and Pudovkin. This exemplifies the range of work qualifying as 'documentary' during the pre-television period. However, the development of a predominantly TV documentary aesthetic since the 1950s brought about a fundamental change. The culturally dominant forms of documentary have developed in a separate context to the films that have been produced within a fine art context, even some of the work produced at the margins of the mainstream of European cinema, such as that of Chantal Ackerman. However, there have occasionally been striking parallels between films produced within these two separate contexts. At the beginning of the new millennium, it is clear that we have reached another such moment, brought about by the availability of inexpensive digital film-making which has revolutionized both traditional documentary practices and the work of contemporary artists. In this moment, it is becoming clear again just how much both practices have in common. From the point of view of aesthetic concerns and procedures, as well as working methods, there are many common features between the forms of documentary practiced in and around television and what I will refer to as artistic practice, which has almost entirely separate means of production and dissemination based around public and art market funding, gallery and festival distribution.

Several common practices lie at the heart of the documentary project. The first is the interview and, more widely, the use of confessional modes of speech. Documentary has for many years used ways of trying to coax people into revelations, showing unexpected intimacies, and particularly revealing moments where people are caught unawares. Recent artistic practice has begun to employ such devices as well. Documentary and artistic practice both try to capture these moments, confronting people in various ways with the meaning of their own lives.

Documentary is also based in a second common practice, but it is more clearly defined as a concept within modernism. It is the notion of the found object, of going out to get footage from somewhere else, something which is already there, rather than creating something for the camera. Documentary is based on going out into the street, getting footage on the fly. Modernists too sought to render ordinary objects into aesthetic objects, or objects of contemplation. Connected with this is the growing documentary concern with the reuse of found footage, or already existing footage. We have seen the dramatic increase in the last few years in the use of archive material of various sorts in documentary practice. On the one hand this can simply be the compilation of historical footage to retell the story of the twentieth century, as seen on the History Channel or UK History. Sometimes it can be used to quite devastating effect as in *Capturing the Friedmans* (2003 Jarecki, A.), which uses the footage shot by the family itself over many years, including the time in which the father and one of the sons were being tried and convicted for child abuse. Throughout, the film remains ambivalent about its characters and the truth of the accusations against them. Again it is a documentary that reveals but does not judge.

The third common aspect is more recent. Increasingly, documentary has tried to combine staged events with the real or the living, especially by combining elements of staging which seem not to be staging. In Channel 4 Television's series, *Faking It*, after a mere four weeks of training, undistinguished individuals try and pretend to be professionals working in some kind of a specialized area. The challenge was simply, would they get away with it or not? This aspect of 'faking' in documentary consists of getting people to pretend to have a skill or a status they do not have. 'Faking' can equally mean that the programme makers contrive to stage events within the ordinary world, whilst trying to cover the pretence in order to discover something about the truth or reality of that world. These are now standard TV documentary practices, providing the basis of the particular outgrowth of documentary known as 'reality TV'. These 'faking' activities clearly involve similar procedures as those of artistic concerns with the hoax, with the fictional construct of the alter ego that many artists have created for themselves, for example, Duchamp's Rrose Sélavy. The implanting of the staged event in the real is another activity that documentary and art practice have in common.

The fourth common aspect is less pronounced in contemporary documentary practice but remains a major concern for art practice. This is a concern with duration. A major element of documentary in the 1960s and 1970s, this is the idea that the event on the screen and the event that was being filmed should be drawn as closely together as possible in terms of their duration. The work of Frederick Wiseman allows events on the screen to unfold as far as possible in the real time it took to record. He extends this concern to refusing to allow extracts to be taken from his films for any further creative purpose, even for the making of a film about his work. Mainstream documentary, especially on television, flirted with this tendency (some extraordinary observational work was done in Northern Ireland for current affairs programmes like World in Action in the late 1960s), but has moved away from this preoccupation, preferring instead to use the editing freedom that has arrived with technologies like Avid or Final Cut Pro. However, an interesting reaction to this pervasive over-cutting is taking place, with documentarists discovering the recent artistic concerns with bringing together presentation time and the real event time, and the possibilities of the gallery space for achieving this. Humphry Trevelyan, of the International Film School Wales, recently demonstrated this by reusing footage he had shot for a conventional documentary on Iran as the basis for a gallery installation that allowed the footage to run at its 'own' length (*Iranian Journey* ZDF/Arte 2000).

More generally the emerging concern with the site specific in artistic practice brings it towards the traditional interests of documentary. It has emerged as a response to the commodification of works of art, and relates to a submerged characteristic of much conventional painting, which was often commissioned and created for specific places. With the re-emergence of the site specific, art practice discovers a sense of place and space, a concern with the concrete, with the things that are unique which belong to one place and which happen in one place. This is the air that documentary breathes, so to speak. Documentary revels in the ordinary, the unconsidered detail or the mundane. Another aspect of this concern is a love for the contingent, that which just chanced to happen. Whether it be the magic moment on a documentary shoot when something truly unexpected occurs in front of the camera, or the particular way that paint behaves on a surface or materials age, this is a shared concern. Anything that happens within a controlled situation but out of the scope of that control is particularly prized both in art and in documentary.

So there are many major aesthetic concerns that documentary shares with a wide range of trends in artistic practice. Looked at purely on the grounds of aesthetics, it would be legitimate to wonder why the predominant forms of documentary and artistic practice do not merge into one another since they have so much in common. But they remain discrete areas of activity. What holds them apart? And what makes dialogue so difficult between them? The answer lies in the different ethical frameworks in which creators undertake their work. Although the aesthetics may be the same, the ethics are very different. Practices and attitudes that are acceptable in one arena may not be acceptable in the other. What is ethically right for one may be wrong for the other. If you want to push the contrast as far as possible, two concerns in documentary practice define the difference: truth and social purpose.

Documentary practitioners are concerned about the truth of what they portray, regarding documentary is a process of reconstituting truth on the screen. Documentary is guided by beliefs about describing something as faithfully and as truthfully as you can, whether it's the truth of the situation, a process or a person. Documentary practice is concerned with reconstituting truth; it may not be literally true, but it tries as far as possible to reconstitute truth within a set of known and knowledged procedures. A documentary film-maker can falsify the duration of an event or even the order in which things happen, but they will do so in the pursuit of what they consider to be a more essential or more important truth. This can be the reality of an individual's psychology, or the reality of a social process. Distortion of events is often justified on the grounds that such and such did happen, but the cameras were not rolling at the time, for example. Despite the appearances of what sometimes passes for documentary on TV, there is an ingrained habit of truthfulness in documentary which is a defining aspect of the practice. It could be said that documentary is concerned with the reconstitution of truth in a formal framework of filmic discourse, and, further, that this reconstitution of truth is its first concern.

The second defining feature of documentary is a sense of social purpose. Documentary is for something. Documentary has a very utilitarian self view. Documentary is about doing. Documentary makers think of themselves as people who want to change the world. They want to change attitudes, they want to get something done, they want to show you something that you would rather not see. This sense of purpose means that documentary seeks as wide an audience as possible and aims to be easily understood. So documentary has been concerned with finding a home in the mass media and welcomed television, when it arrived, as its ideal home. Documentary is concerned with getting out there as much as possible, getting seen and finding its way on to television, finding its way into cinemas and into schools, where people go, into what used to be quaintly called 'meetings of people'. Documentary attempts to enact that social purpose as much as possible within a mass media setting, if it can get away with it.

Artistic practice does not have the same priorities. Most artistic practice is not primarily concerned with defining a truth. It may well discover a way to truth, but it begins with a fundamentally different motivation: the desire to create a new object, a desire to see and create anew. The project of creating something that did not exist before is a crucial difference of emphasis. To claim the vocation of an artist is to set out to make something new. That is the prime motivation and the discovery of truth is secondary to it. The documentary vocation has a different governing perspective. The discovery and communication of truth is what motivates a documentary maker, and the desire to make something new comes as a consequence of it.

Allied with the fundamental artistic motivation of making something new is the idea of the aesthetic thrill, the idea of producing something whose sensual aspect is important. Much documentary making is defiantly anti-sensual. Beauty of composition, fluency of sound design, elegance of construction are all categories that documentary tends to shun because they imply an excess of artifice. Such was the critique of Errol Morris's *Thin Blue Line* (1988) when it was first released. Why, critics asked, did Morris not release as soon as he could this film about the wrongful conviction of Randall Adams for the murder of a Dallas policeman? Interviews within it clearly demonstrated that the police had presumed his guilt from the outset, and another man effectively confesses to the murder. So why wait to craft the documentary with its close-ups of details of reconstructed events and carefully balanced testimony? After all, Adams had to wait three years on death row for Morris's devastating film to be released and to reveal this miscarriage of justice. Such are the dilemmas of the committed documentary maker. Morris's film has influenced a whole generation of film-makers since, of course, and its adventurous aesthetic drew more attention to Adams' case than any routine TV investigation of a miscarriage of justice would have done. But the question remains: why would a committed documentarist spend time on aesthetic effects rather than getting the message 'out there'.

Overwhelmingly, artistic activity does not face such dilemmas. Aesthetics are its core business and its social purpose, not a suspicious piece of decoration that can obstruct more important work. Much artistic activity is not goal driven in the way that most documentaries are. It is exploratory rather than goal directed, which makes all those funding application forms so tricky to fill in. The forms require the statement of goals; they could have been devised by the people who commission documentaries (as they often have been). Nothing, apart from money and celebrity, impels artistic practice into the mass media. The idea of 'selling out' is a common theme within criticism and personal attack alike in the 'art world'. But there is no equivalent 'documentary world' in which such a critique would be relevant, and even if there were, selling out would be applied very sparingly rather than to everything that gained a mainstream audience. Documentary has a close, if not over-cosy, relationship with the mainstream of mass culture. Artistic practice has a more antagonistic, critical or even hostile attitude to the mass media.

Documentary and art may have many procedures in common, but creators working in these fields operate within different ethical frameworks. The working practices of documentary, and in particular its ethical concerns of truth and social purpose, have kept the two groups firmly apart. They talk different talk, they drink in different pubs. They look to very different institutions for their funding and they go to different spaces for their audiences. But they do share one basic intention: to shift view points, to shock, to reveal, to disturb preoccupations, to make consumers think and feel in a way that they have not before. So a rapprochement has long been possible, particularly as both practices are fast-changing, fluid and dynamic. For art and documentary alike, styles and approaches quickly become dated. Both are restless in the pursuit of their chosen goals.

Recently, documentary's search for truth has brought it closer to many of the concerns of artistic practice, and documentary has begun to appear in gallery spaces. Film-makers like Isaac Julien have reinvented themselves as artists working with film in gallery spaces. The reason is clear: there is something of an ethical crisis playing itself out in the arena of documentary film-making. The documentary notion of fidelity to reality has become more of a problem. To understand this is to see that we may well have arrived at the point where the ethical concerns of documentary and art are converging.

This documentary ethic of fidelity to reality remains strong, even when documentary makers set up an event to see what happens, which is more common, especially in television. They still aim to show what actually happened as faithfully as possible within the conventions of their media. The nature of these conventions is important. A key example is the classic 1971 BBC television series, directed by Paul Watson, *The Family*. This is a utilitarian documentary series that aimed to show what goes on within a working-class family in Britain. The series was distinguished by the relationship between shooting and broadcast. The first week of shooting was edited in week two and broadcast in week three, whilst filming was still taking place. The Wilkins family were therefore able to see how they were being received, and to reply to their critics. Given this speed of production and unusual public visibility, the form of the programmes was extremely careful to guarantee as much fidelity to reality as possible.

Early in the first episode, we see the youngest son of Mr and Mrs Wilkins being upbraided for his poor school report. The conversation was obviously a long one, and it is edited extensively. But it is transparently edited, with short fades to black at every break, so the event is condensed, but the integrity of the event is still gestured towards very visibly. Condensing the event not only intensifies it, but it also introduces an abrupt and dramatic transition. The parents begin by trying to encourage their son to acknowledge that he has been, in the words of the report, 'lazy'. They point out that he is clever and could do better than his father (a shopkeeper). But their own insecurities gradually come to the fore and they become more hectoring. Then the sudden transition takes the interaction away from verbal exchange. We cut to the son in floods of tears and the parents, realizing that they have gone too far, trying to comfort him. The editing shortens the sequence, shows very explicitly where the cutting has taken place, and heightens the dramatic development of the exchange.

However, there is no explicit judgement made by the film in this sequence. We are not told what to think, we are not told that this is bullying, we are not told that this is humiliating the young son, and we are not told that the parents are entirely justified. There is no particular moral position taken in relation to what we have seen in this footage. Events are shown for our inspection. A viewer can feel sympathy for the child and hostility to the parents or sympathy for all parties. The scene is extremely emotional and probably typical of scenes experienced by many members of the viewing audience. But judgement is left to that audience.

Judgement is avoided out of a respect for the event itself, which is central to the way in which documentary constructs its material. This respect for the event is so marked in classic documentary procedures that it is sometimes tempting to think that there is more respect for the integrity of the event itself than there is respect for the people involved in the event. However, respect for the persons involved has to be a major concern for documentary, if it is being constructed for a very indiscriminate mass media, like television. As the responses to Watson's *The Family* demonstrated in 1971, the parameters governing reactions to a medium like television are much looser than those which govern an awful lot of gallery practices. It is much less easy to predict what reactions might be to screening material on television than to presenting them in a gallery context.

Such concerns of fidelity to reality are central to documentary, but relatively marginal in most artistic practices, to the point of being a non-issue most of the time. However, to be caught faking something whilst claiming not to (even by default) is the worst thing that a documentary film-maker can be accused of. To be discovered to have invented something and claimed that it is real is the end of the line for a professional documentarist. In Germany, for Michael Born, the faking of news footage led to a period of imprisonment. For Carlton TV in Britain, the faking of a film about the Columbian drugs business, *The Connection*, led to a £4 million fine. The film-maker, Marc de Beaufort, retreated from film-making to run a restaurant in Chile.

These revelations at the end of the 1990s provoked a crisis in documentary production. A press outcry followed these and other attempts to compromise the core documentary value of fidelity to the real. This crystallized into a sustained campaign against the makers of prime-time documentary or factual programmes about people going about their ordinary business, about traffic wardens, about people passing their driving tests and so on. It emerged that they were getting their ordinary people to restage events, to do things again for the camera. The newspapers claimed that this footage was in some sense faked and then being passed off as the real thing. Instead of confronting the relationship between the camera, the documentarist and the documentary subject, television documentary retreated from the debate.[1]

No TV documentarist involved in the debate mounted an argument along these lines:

> What else do you expect us to be able to do? Everybody who we will be filming will know quite a lot about television documentaries. They will have seen documentaries, they will know something about how they are made, because nowadays most people have got access to cameras of their own. People are not the naïve people they used to be. They are not the sort of people you can expect just to ignore the presence of the camera. Things have changed

for us documentary filmmakers, and we have to come to terms with the complicity of our subjects in the filming process.

Documentary and television at the end of the last century did not make such a case. Instead they retreated from that debate and rethought their practices. What they came up with was a number of documentary formats in which people were faced with challenges in which the fictional nature of the set up of the factual film-making was made very explicit. Reality TV, currently the dominant form of factual television, is a response to these accusations of fakery in television documentary in Britain in the late 1990s. One trend takes it towards *Big Brother*, towards the notion of putting ordinary people (or perhaps less than ordinary people) into an artificial space and facing them with the challenge of getting on with each other, yet also talking about each other all the time. Another trend is formats which put people through a process of therapy or transformation. Examples include Channel 4's *Brat Camp*, BBC3's *The House of Tiny Tearaways*, where problem families are taken through a therapeutic process to produce a more sociable result. Others, like Channel 4's *Beauty and the Geek*, take young adults, with self-acknowledged social defects, through a competitive learning process. In all these cases, the artificiality of the situation is built into the very reason for watching these factual programmes.

Reality television enabled documentary to find its place in the mass media as a semi-entertainment format. Nevertheless, documentary can and does go on making claims to fidelity to reality. It simply makes explicit the fact that the reality in question has been set up for the programme, and this is known by the participants and the audience alike. Truth emerges elsewhere in these formats, in the psychological truths that are revealed about the personalities involved. This is an artificial reality in which the truth about people still comes through, whether it is the truth about family interaction, the personalities in the *Big Brother* house or the capacity of individuals to transform themselves. These may be confessional truths or exhibitionist truths, but their status is clear from the explicit nature of the format concerned.

Beyond the peak hour entertainment of reality TV, another trend in documentary elected to go on making the same sorts of films, to go on confronting the real, but crucially to build in an acknowledgement of the place of the camera and the film maker within the film itself. Nick Broomfield has made a career out of this, by building himself into his own films. He always adopts the same persona in his films, slightly clumsy and hapless. This adoption of an incompetent persona is how the truthfulness of his documentaries is established. The film-maker pretends to reveal a bit about himself, to show himself in not an entirely good light, so that viewers can feel that they have seen some kind of truth about the making of the documentary. This supposed insight then stands as an affidavit or a guarantee of the truthfulness of the larger film in which that footage appears.

This, then, is the current state of documentary film-making within TV. Of course, it will transmute before very long. But there are two conclusions to draw from this about the potential relation between documentary and art. The crisis around the key concept of fidelity to reality in documentary has brought the two closer together. On the one hand, the new-found emphasis on performance and pretence in documentary brings it in touch with a rich seam in modern and postmodern artistic practice. On the other hand, some documentarists have begun to use the spaces developed by artistic practice to rediscover some of the ethical values of fidelity to reality and respect for individual documentary subjects.

Pretence, simulation, faking, reproduction, copying are all things that documentary has tried to push into the background. Artistic practices of various sorts revel in such procedures, regarding them as part of what and who we are and how we live in contemporary society. One of the great things about art since at least the moment of Dada is that it has realized that within the era of mass media certain things are central to how we live our lives. Pretence, role playing and imposture are things we all do, as a part of everyday life. They are not to be avoided or got beyond. It is a part of what and who we are and how we live. Reproduction, copying, simulation and homage are major parts of modern life. This is the lesson of Cindy Sherman's photos. Pretence comes with the electronic media and all the digital processes that are part of contemporary urban industrial life. For artistic practice, the notion of fidelity to the concrete reality is not an overarching ethical stance as it is for documentary, but instead simply a particular procedure available for use, which produces particular effects. Fidelity to reality is just one technique in an arsenal of techniques for confronting the viewer with something that simply didn't exist in the world before.

This perception provides a new space for documentary: the gallery. A number of film-makers like Cahal McLaughlin, Humphry Trevelyan and Isaac Julien have discovered that the gallery allows a radically different form of display. It is not linear and univocal as a conventional documentary is. Multiple screens can be used, and multiple audio spaces can be created. Footage of interviews or events can be run and repeated without the need for cutting. Viewers can move between footage, sounds and voices at a pace that they, rather than film-makers, dictate. The gallery provides the possibility of a floating and provisional point of view on the events or people who have been filmed. This floating point of view restores the possibility of an honesty in relation to material. The gallery provides a space for rethinking the whole ethical notion of fidelity to reality.

Note
1. Ellis, J. 'Documentary and Truth on Television: The Crisis of 1999', in Corner, J. and Rosenthal, A. *New Challenges for Documentary* (2nd ed.), Manchester University Press, 2005.

COLLABORATIONS AND TECHNOLOGIES

Stella Bruzzi (interlocutor), Gideon Koppel, Jane and Louise Wilson in conversation

In this panel discussion with Stella Bruzzi (interlocutor), Gideon Koppel and Jane and Louise Wilson, technology is examined as part of the creative process. Collaborations between artists, film-makers and their subjects are explored.

Stella Bruzzi recently completed the second edition of *New Documentary* (2006) and is currently writing a study of the seminal television documentary series *Seven Up*. Gideon Koppel's work as a film-maker is exhibited in a wide variety of formats: from the film installation for fashion label Comme des Garcons screened at the 1998 Florence Biennale to the acclaimed documentary series *Undressed* (1997) for Channel 4/Canal+/WDR. He is currently working on a feature documentary based on *a sketchbook for The Library Van*. Jane and Louise Wilson exhibit video projections, photographs taken during the filming process, and three-dimensional sculptures. Their work explores power, surveillance and paranoia. Their installations, for example, *Dream Time* (2001) and *Broken Time* (2005), explore the psychology and architectural language surrounding certain buildings, as well as investigating sites of political power.

SB
Jane and Louise Wilson will discuss their work, focusing on their latest film, *Dream Time*, and Gideon Koppel will refer to a couple of his shorter pieces to contextualize his work. Let them introduce themselves.

LW
Dream Time was filmed in 2001 at the Russian Cosmodrome in Kazakhstan. Just briefly, to fill you in on our background, Jane and I did an MA in Fine Art at Goldsmith's College (1990–92) and have been based in London ever since. We show with the Lisson Gallery here in London and the 303 Gallery in New York. Until now, our work has mostly been seen in galleries or museums, so this conference is a new context for us.

JW
I would like to add that we often create installation work rather than single screen or film projection, but this piece was created after we had filmed in Moscow and Star City. We filmed

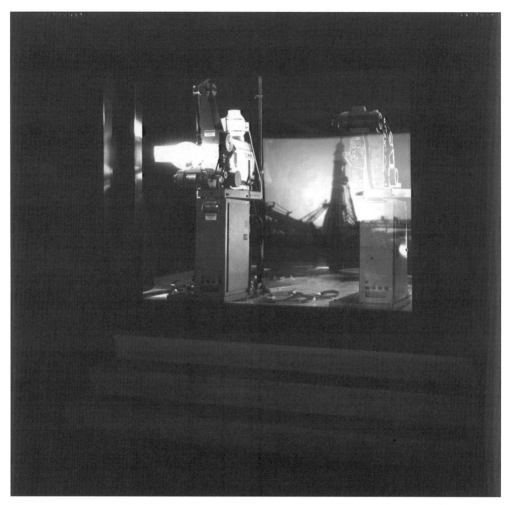

Dream Time, 2001, 35mm film

another piece in Kazakhstan, called *Proton, Unity, Energy, Blizzard,* which is named after all the launch sites we documented. *Dream Time* was a more speculative venture because we documented parts of a rocket being assembled. We then went back and filmed the launch itself.

LW

That was certainly a different sort of challenge for us: we were looking at a media event, as well as being involved in it. The main subject was the *Dream Time* rocket – the first American-Russian manned space mission to set up the international space station in October 2001.

It was overcast on the day the rocket was set to lift off, but five minutes before the launch, the mist began to clear. This wasn't a classic shot of a rocket traversing the sky – it was more of a blur before it vanished into the clouds. But we quite enjoyed that.

Dream Time, 2001, 35mm film

Dream Time is about the launch of the Soyuz™ rocket. In the opening shot, you see scientists looking through blueprints. Nothing is done on computer — it is all done on blueprints, even the design for the solar panels fitted onto one of the rockets. It is a huge sophisticated catapult, but it is also a mechanical process that uses a lot of fuel.

We were looking at this and other edited pieces on a full screen with digital media and a digital result. But it was shot on film and for the final installation where we showed this work, we used a 35mm projection. 35mm projectors are mechanical and cumbersome and it was something we wanted to convey in the installation — this feel of the mechanical and the analogue.

GK

I showed a piece of work called *sketchbook for The Library Van* which I was uncertain about showing in this context because it was not made as 'a film' for screening. It was funded by the Film Council as a pilot for a feature-length film, *The Library Van*. This 'pilot' wasn't intended as a trailer, taster or neat synthesis of the film. On the contrary — the aim was to create an alternative text in which the characters of the film were isolated from that landscape which is integral to their lives and stories. Each individual was filmed against a simple white backdrop, reminiscent of Richard Avedon's penetrating portraits *In the American West* — portraiture without romanticism or contrived drama — a direct and frank exchange between the subject

Sketchbook for The Library Van

Comme des Garçons installation, 1998 Florence Biennale

and the camera. The compositions are simple and the image is detailed, revealing the physicality and gesture of the characters, almost with the brutality of a Lucien Freud painting.

I guess that often my initial references are paintings – I originally studied mathematics and many years later did a postgraduate at the Slade School of Fine Art, working with the performance artist Stuart Brisley. The other short pieces of work that I have shown today represent two other 'worlds' I work in – an award-winning commercial I made for the NSPCC and a film I made for Rei Kawakubo as part of the Comme des Garçons exhibition at The Florence Biennale. I thought they might be relevant because both pieces involve interesting relationships with technology, which I was told would be central to the discussion today.

SB

I would like to start with a question that Michael Renov ended with – what do artists have to gain from documentary? Gideon and Louise are both very clear that even if the material is factual, they are not making documentaries. So I would like you to talk about the process that alters that: is it a question of how you look at the material or is it a question of how the material is received? How is this contextualized and what alters that fundamental relationship with the document?

JW

As artists, screening a single-screen film is not reflective of everything we do. We are very aware of documentary film-making, but it is not something that we see ourselves as doing. We see ourselves as artists who happen to document things. Does that make us documentarists?

Our compulsion, in very early works, has often been to look at non visible, abandoned or disused places. We are very conscious when filming, particularly with something like *Star City*, not to tamper or interfere too much with what was there – if it is still a memorial site you should not treat it as a neutral backdrop. We can be aware of what we are recording, and have respect for it, but we also want to communicate this from a respectful distance.

LW

Documentary has a myriad of descriptions and experiences. And as an installation piece, it can involve an even greater physical encounter.

GK

It seems to me that when you look at the work of The Lumière Brothers...the event of filming the workers leaving the factory and then screening the material back to them that evening...the origins of documentary film can seem to be akin to ideas found in contemporary performance and installation.

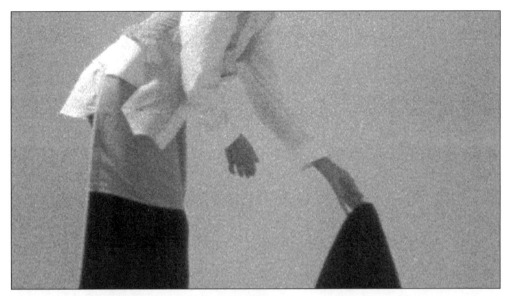

Comme des Garçons installation, 1998 Florence Biennale

NSPCC *Open Your Eyes* commercial

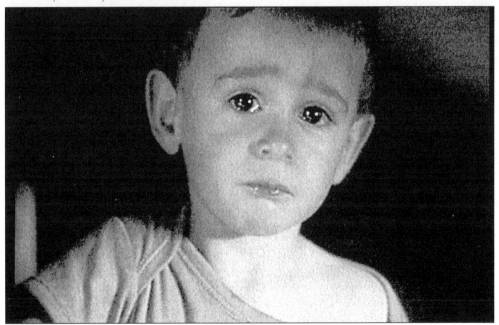

LW

Another artist, Gillian Wearing, refers to the significant influence of *42 UP* (a series following the lives of children every seven years, from the age of seven, which began as *7 UP*) on her work, and is something that we grew up with as well.

Broken Time, The Great North Run

SB
Gideon, your film, *sketchbook for a Library Van*, is very people-based, whereas I was talking to Louise yesterday about *Broken Time* and also about *Dream Time* and about liking/working within architectural space and with architecture. What is that relationship between you and the subjects? A part of this discussion is about collaboration, but is that collaboration between you and the people or objects filmed crucial to your work?

JW
I guess initially we started off using each other as subjects and then gradually that evolved into something else.

Broken Time, The Great North Run

LW

Broken Time and *Dream Time* are about physicality and the way that figures are framed in an urban environment.

GK

I guess that in many ways I am autistic about the world. I am not chummy or chatty with the people in front of the camera. I made a film for the BBC about a fashion designer and I cannot say that even for a minute of the year I spent with him, did I feel any empathy for him. When I am making a film, I am primarily trying to evoke my experience of the world – perhaps a sense of the transference and counter-transference.

SB

How are you evoking your experience with that person?

GK

I don't know. You can sit in a landscape, look at the vista and think 'this is just fantastic'. You can feel the warmth of the air, you can inhale the sweet smell of dried grass...but how do you evoke those sensations, that experience, in an image? You don't need to have a smell pumping out in the auditorium. You might frame a piece of grass that is gently moving in the wind and slow it down even further in camera – the languid movement suggesting an equivalent moment of contemplation. Then maybe you introduce the sound of the sea...it's got nothing to do with the actuality of the landscape – rather, it is a kind of translation. The choice of medium becomes critical when you work in that idiom. It seems to me that film images [rather than video] have more possibilities for evoking the intimacy and contemplation I suggested in this example of the pastoral landscape.

JW

You are probably having more of a relationship with the rocket than you are with some of the people. It is important for us to shoot with film because we shoot a lot of stills and photographic work which takes place during filming. I agree that within this situation it is immaterial whether we screen our films on DVD or 35mm, but when you actually exhibit your work, it is important to return to that materiality and to what you are essentially interested in.

LW

The example you gave about a blade of grass and trying to describe a whole experience by evoking a certain sound is interesting. You mentioned that would work on film. However, if you

Sketchbook for The Library Van

look at the late 1960s and early 1970s, gallery and performance-based work was all shot on video. There was something about the reality of that meaning, and about making it feel real and physical that meant it was right it should be on video. Film had the immediacy that was essential for that kind of physical encounter, and we sometimes forget what those mediums once signified.

JW
Coming back to the question of subject, there is a much broader sense now of what is a subject, of how you can be subjective and what subject to use.

SB
In a catalogue from the end of the 1990s, Jane and Louise say that they differentiate themselves from film-makers because they do not impose anything, not even a narrative and respond only to the material that they find. Also, both Louise and Gideon emphasized the fact that they do not see their work as being linear. Can I ask you to develop those ideas as well as differentiating between how you see your work and more conventional forms of film-making? Can we then start with the idea of not imposing something?

Sketchbook for The Library Van

LW
On a very obvious level, a lot of these installations are shown on a loop and run continuously. *Broken Time* was screened as a single work but shown as a two-screen work. When it was exhibited it was shown with one screen starting at the beginning and halfway through on the other screen. So there was a constant overlap where you were at the beginning of the race, or at the end. It had a loop feel about it and in that sense it is non-linear. *Dream Time* and *Broken Time* document an event in a fairly linear way too: the motivation was a beginning, middle and an end, culminating in a rocket launch. But perhaps there is a sense that it is non-linear because there is no direct voice-over or narrative. *Broken Time* ends in an interior space in a car park and not just at the end of the race, whereas *Dream Time* ends in the interior space of the cosmodrome. I know it is a small point, but the motivation is essentially that these works are shown on a loop and that you can encounter them at any point.

SB
For me that is what completely alters the way you view it. So you do not view it as a linear narrative at all — you watch it regardless of wherever the original event is because you are being invited to look at it in a fragmented way.

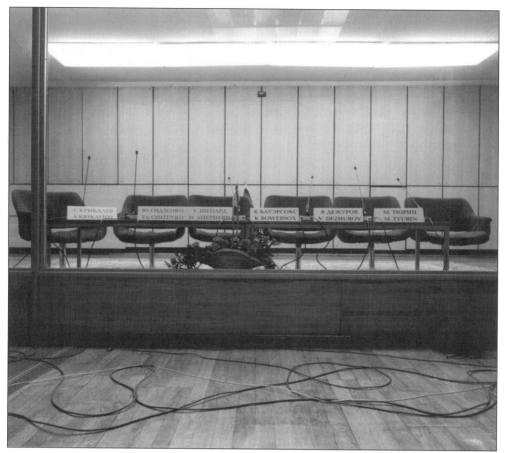

Dream Time, press conference, 2001, C-print on aluminium with aluminium edging, 180x180 cm

JW

Even with something like *Broken Time* we were much more compelled by the concrete in the buildings around us than we were by the runners. Obviously the runners were part of it, but our main desire was to capture that concrete space. Gideon has said he was removed from his subjects but it is something that we were much more interested to see.

LW

Similarly with the *sketchbook* piece yesterday — which was an hour long — do you feel that if you came into that work at any one point, you would know what was going on?

GK

I never thought that I would edit it together and show it as a linear piece, although when I saw it yesterday, I felt there was a kind of natural end to it. While I would like people to drift in and out of the piece, I also noticed in the screening yesterday, that when anybody left, my impulse was to get up and tell them to get back in...I was tempted to lock the door. I suppose part of

Stasi City, 1997, 2 Laserdiscs, installation dimensions variable

it is wanting people to have a certain kind of immersion in that world on screen, to stop listening to the words and fall into the musicality of it.

JW
Immersion is interesting because sometimes you miss the extreme choreography of what the film-makers were shooting.

LW
There is something about being able to sit down and make a real commitment to something important, and this work was an hour long for a reason. It was not something that was running on a three-minute loop. I think it is more of a journey — not a linear description or talking about a linear narrative — but an idea of a journey.

SB
Yes, instinctively we think of a journey as being linear, but, in fact, most journeys aren't. Thank you. Now can I ask for questions from the audience.

Jacqueline Maingard, University of Bristol
I am curious because I wanted to know about Gideon's next project. You said this is a pilot for a fiction film, and I wonder how different it is, what it is about and how it acts as a pilot?

GK
I guess that I don't know whether *The Library Van* will be fiction or documentary...it looks like the financiers are also now confused. It will be fundamentally different to *a sketchbook* because I will film people within their environments...and over a period of six months. At the same time I hope that it will retain a sense of 'the meditative' quality present in the *sketchbook*. I know that I shouldn't say this but I do not know what the film will be — one of the exhilarating dynamics of a project like this for me is that I will discover the 'film' when I make it.

Michael Uwemedimo, Roehampton University
I want to offer an observation and ask a few questions about the relationship and exchange between documentary and art. From the practice that I am involved in, Vision Machine, we view our projects as creating and generating a universe of materials. So the project we are doing in Indonesia, with hundreds of hours of testimony from survivors and perpetrators of the 1965–66 genocide also includes performances and documents: a universe of materials that can be resolved in different instances into different forms. It exists as an archive that can be equally available to academics, activists and artists. Or the archive can be an installation or a series of testimonies, or else resolve itself into a linear documentary. I am just wondering if any of you here have that feeling of creating a universe that can resolve itself. It is not just documentary, or an artist's film: there is mobility.

JW
I would agree with you that there is mobility there, but seeing things in terms of using a multi-screen, or not, has been a large part of our work for fifteen years. It is not just something that can be spatialized or archived or documented, it is something that we are involved in, in terms of a formalizing language process. Sometimes it is dangerous to just see things in those terms. I feel that video has a great accessibility to it and it is a great freedom to actually use and manipulate it. But on another level, it is just another backdrop.

MU
It doesn't have to be arbitrary because the different instances will frame the work in different ways.

JW
I feel like there are other difficulties we encountered in terms of installation.

LW
It is interesting because I can see the main incentive and drive behind the work was actually the making of the archive. They are just different approaches.

Jini Rawlings, University of Westminster and artist
I wanted to come back to something Michael Renov was saying in his keynote speech about ethics. You mentioned the documentarist having an ethical stance and relating it to the respect that you have for the building as a memorial. I just wondered if you could say a bit more about this.

Michael Renov
Thank you for raising that because I was thinking along the same lines listening to what was said earlier. I found myself with both *Broken Time* and *Dream Time* and certainly with the *sketchbook for The Library Van*, noticing (maybe I'm just eccentric) the people do exert a certain kind of pull and it creates what in documentary studies we call epistophilia, meaning a kind of desire and curiosity. Sometimes it is just an intellectual curiosity, but I think that seeing what other people are like, inspires a certain curiosity. You may say that you are as drawn to the physical, the 'objecthood' of the world or the texture of the stone, but in this case, the viewer was amazed by all the details in *Dream Time*, and there was a tremendous intellectual curiosity

about it. That does not give you an ethical dimension, except that I think people, rather than objects, exert a fascination on other people. So the ethical question really shifts – we must ask, 'What kind of responsibility do you bear for that other?' I'm interested by the language artists use to describe that level of responsibility.

JW

When I think back to having an obligation to the building, particularly in relation to this piece of work, it was also because we did not want to manipulate the physical objects that were left there. The Stasi had smashed everything and left quickly. Also, we were opening doors that they were finding keys for that had not been opened for ten years. Going into this space and pointing a camera was really about capturing that moment of the object, not the person.

MR

I appreciate that, but when Gideon said he wanted to lock the door and not let anybody out, to me it is different because it is about these people's lives. If I walk out, I feel I am walking out on a person and a person's life.

GK

I am beginning to discover that my own idiom as a film-maker is to use the camera to put a frame around 'a fragment' or 'moment' and wait...to allow things to emerge and evolve within that construct. This seems to be contrary to the often used notion in documentary of 'following' a subject.

MR

Can I introduce the Barthesian notion of the punctum? If we're following along with the studium you are right: following action was what direct cinema was all about, and it is the reason why those cameras were so good. That is why the Nagras were so good, but that was all about the studium. The point I was trying to make earlier was that I am more likely to find points of engagement, or epiphanous moments, in relation to people.

Documentary cameraman, Bafta winner and artist

I see the contemplative in Gideon's and Jane and Louise's work, but when I hear them talking, they also provide the narrative, the documentary side. At the same time, listening to Gideon speak about how he would reflect landscape with a blade of a grass, suggests that contemplation is often missing in documentary. However, even if there is no narrative in documentary, even if it is just observational, we bring the thoughts of the viewer to it. In Gideon and Louise and Jane's pieces, we can bring what we love in literature or in the cinema to the piece. Our mind is carried along, and that is the real contrast I feel between the two worlds. In television, people try to enter it and they will never succeed because the broadcast and the commercial pressure demand a certain political content to what is projected. If we pursue documentary as an art, that is fantastic because it means there will be no politics involved. I don't know if you follow me there.

MR

Up until the end, when you said you want to eliminate politics. I have a little trouble with that, and I hear what you are saying about the contemplative. But the contemplative, I would argue, has never been entirely absent from the documentary. Like I said, the televisual introduces a different urgency.

LW

It's just a different, very specific, language

JW

Or there's a different goal towards it, which is why there is a commissioning element which is your impetus to create. You're not answering to anybody really.

MR

In Claude Lanzmann's nine-and-a-half-hour film, *Shoah* (1993), there are a lot of moments for contemplation and a lot of empty space.

Dick Fontaine, National Film and Television School

I find this characterization of documentary and television journalism objectionable, particularly in the last question. It means that nobody would watch documentaries and certainly not Sergei Dvortsevoy's films (who would characterize himself as a documentary maker). One of the things I have noticed – and this is by no means true of all film work in galleries and installation – is that it does not take its role seriously. It says 'this is our prerogative – I am an artist and screw you'. I think this debate ought to be more to do with that, than with an attack on television.

JW

We are not trying to be elitist if that is what you're implying, but I can understand why you might feel that way. I think it is because we are all struggling with the same question that you are, i.e., how to define what a documentary is. What does it combine? What does it represent? Lots of different people and lots of different voices are participating in this discussion, and it is not something we are prioritizing or being hierarchical about because it exists in galleries.

DF

Can I ask you a very specific question to do with your film about the launch (which is fantastic: the end bit was lovely)? When you were talking about analogue versus digital, why do you use the split screen, and what was the motivation for going into that split screen universe every so often?

LW

Very simply, Jane and I started working with four-way splits – four separate installation screens. It was a spatial work because screen 1 and screen 2 would meet in a corner, and diagonally opposite, screen 3 and screen 4 would meet in another corner. We were editing like that with screens 1, 2, 3, 4, and we were beginning to see we were making pictures that could exist as a whole image. While thinking about that, I guess the four-way split just developed. It was something that we worked on as four separate screens but then realized that it worked just as well on one screen.

JW
I think it was also partly our own discomfort with just seeing a single image, a single shot, because often we experience or like to try and see film through multiple perspectives and different peripheral visions and spaces.

Adam Kossoff, film-maker and artist
There is a missing element in this discussion which is the idealism behind documentaries – the need to get closer to the subject. It suddenly occurred to me while watching *Dream Time*, that it enabled me to understand Jane and Louise's work. By filming something in order to get physically close, there is an emphasis placed on the physicality of the work. This is a documentary ideal, but it has been proved in documentary theory at least to be an impossible idea. When I saw the shot of the astronaut through the glass window, I realized that we can't actually be there. This impossibility and ideal need to be looked at.

Elizabeth Cowie, University of Kent
I just wanted to pick up on a couple of things relating to the idea of what it means to produce work using recorded reality, and to ask if the issue of documentary may be a red herring. Could we talk about recording reality, and how you use it? There has been some shifting ground on the traditional conventions and assumptions of documentary film-making. Why is this changing now, and why do we talk about digital rather than video? What does it mean to contemplate or to know? For example, following 9/11, Channel 4 broadcast a short piece in the news slot the next day. But because it was the wrong material for that news slot, it was 'transgressive': you would have had to have seen the images from the day before in order to experience the reality of the piece the day after. So how is actuality being used?

JW
That is a big question. I remember Louise was reflecting about the first artists who worked with videos (Vito Acconci, for example) and how people used it, and used themselves as performers and protagonists, and created a sculptural space around themselves. But they were not documenting a life, or representing a key moment or an historical occasion. We are like Vito Acconci – we perform in front of something and run along with it as a documentation of ideas.

MR
When you talked about 9/11, I was thinking of the first images I saw of London after the bombings, taken with camera phones. I was in Los Angeles and had just left London where I stayed in Tavistock Square (the site of one of the bombings). Those camera phone images offered me an entry point into something that was happening elsewhere in the world, and as you say, that is part of the kind of burden of representation that artists who use this work and these technologies now bear.

GK
While art more or less creates its own moral constructs, the notion of documentary has largely been subsumed into television...so that the term 'documentary' has become more associated with the 'recording' of fact, than the evocation of a world.

Alisa Lebow, University of the West of England

The cultural and institutional context of documentary film-making has not yet been explored. Perhaps there is a cultural reason why so many people are declaring themselves to be artists, and not documentarians. And talking about the authority of documentary, are we regaining a notion of aura? What happens to these so-called images of actuality when they enter into this rarefied art world?

LW

When you mention aura, I automatically think of authenticity. There is an argument that galleries are almost like churches, and that we approach them with a similar sense of reverence, contemplation and meditation, all of which adds to the notion of aura.

AL

But is it seen as art by the art world, or does it suddenly become so because of veneration, critique and, ultimately, marketing? Suddenly something becomes an object d'art whereas outside in the real world, it is something you piss in. It needs to be thought through.

JW

I think it always has been thought through.

John Ellis

This discussion indicates that there aren't two camps at all, just people struggling with a relatively new perception: the act of filming or rather the desire to film, and then the desire to show things on screen. Conflict arises when you enter into a deeper-than-usual human relationship within a documentary. Then it becomes a problem: do you want to show this stuff, and why do you want to show this stuff? Why does this other person want to make a spectacle of themselves? Is it right that having made this film, we should then make a spectacle of the result, and ourselves within that?

SB

More questions than answers. That is how it should be. Thank you panellists and audience.

Is It Art?

Gail Pearce

Until the Truth or Dare conference and this ensuing book, I did not define my work as documentary or myself as a documentary film-maker. Now I am less sure. This chapter examines how art and documentary film can collide with each other and redefine themselves in moving image work. Using a selection of my own work as examples, I explore some of the definitions that documentary seems to collect, including those by Bill Nichols and Julia Lesage.

In the infinite number of binary positions that are possible in the positioning of art and documentary, theory and practice, creating one between moving image as art and moving image as documentary now seems more artificial and constructed. I hope to recategorize my material and to integrate the concepts of art and documentary.

I have been a practising artist for over thirty years and have flirted with using documentary as part of my practice. Looking back it becomes obvious that my work has reflected many of the obsessions of the late twentieth century, particularly feminism, psychoanalysis and identity politics. I have always used drawing as a starting point, with sculpture, photography, animation, film-making and video making following. Now the computer is an integral part of whatever I make, and interaction is central to the work, thanks to digital software and hardware. I notice how developments in technologies have impacted on my documentary practice.

As an artist I was often unaware of the debates that were attached to documentary film-making. I created film and video work that included subjects ranging from small socially aware projects, for example, the art education of Latin American immigrant children, to more personal projects focusing on my family. More recently, I can reassess my work in the context of a number of categories. I used moving image to create dramas that explore identity and family history, animations that question relationships within the family and biases within art history, documentary that I now realize falls into both ethnography and the avant-garde, as well as, more recently, installations which explore space and place, thereby adding a further dimension linked to documentary. Using Super 8, Hi-band Umatic and more obscure formats, I have also created home movie footage, a valuable archive resource for future projects and an integral part of many documentaries, particularly those made by artists.

In my exploration of the ideas underpinning documentary, I began to uncover aspects of documentary in moving image that were unknown to me. If documentary and art come out of the same creative source I want to understand whether and if separation occurred. Where modern art was moving beyond realism at the end of the nineteenth century, most photography and the moving image were attempting to capture reality more precisely. Photographic reality did not aim to be always sharply focused or in extreme detail, it often looked to painting for its inspiration. Images were dependent on the technological inventions of the time, ways of seeing were generally being contextualized in new ways. Painters were able to take their easels outside, were forced to work quickly in oil paint and contributed to Impressionism. The first Impressionist exhibition was in 1874, by which time photography was well established. The importance of Impressionism and the effect of artists being able to be freed from the studio and be independent, representing their personal thoughts and aims, resulted in creativity being redefined. This definition is in constant flux and is a vital part of the modern movement. Georges Peillex suggested that

> Much time was to pass before the public would admit that a picture is first of all a painting, and not a picture of something.[1]

Documentaries have had to contend with similar responses. Abstraction and lack of narrative continue to challenge audiences. However, cameras allowed daily life to be recorded quickly and with great enthusiasm, and in the USA film was a rival to, and a progression from, the extremely popular stereographic images of travel that had invaded the late-nineteenth-century sitting room. People liked looking at the world from the safety of their home. The stereograph was used for both entertainment and education, sometimes at the same time, allowing people to discover they were curious about geography, history, industries and science. Education was highly valued and linked to technologies, the stereograph becoming fashionable as well as educational. Judith Babbitts writes:

> Stereographs illustrate the extraordinary prestige and ideological legitimacy of a *way* of acquiring knowledge in a given historical time.[2]

Everyday images were being marketed and everyday life, particularly the unknown and foreign, was seen as worthy of recording. Bill Nichols writes, 'Every film is a documentary' because of its ability to reflect culture in more than one way.[3] Historically, although we might be tempted to define all early cinema as documentary, that would be to oversimplify. While examining the past, I tried to establish how art and documentary were seen in relation to each other. My work hovered between definitions of either and both. Catherine Russell writes on early film forms,

> ...the dominant mode of film practice before 1907 was the actuality. Actualities were short films shot around the world, nominally 'unstaged', although many were documents of performances, dances, processions, and parades.[4]

Strangers Vanessa Brown

Strangers, filmed in 1988, is closest in my work to a documentary. It was a low-budget short film about three women living in Antigua, one from Domenica, one from Guyana and one who was Antiguan. The outsiders, or 'strangers' as everyone called them, came for work, while the Antiguan had always wanted to emigrate to the UK. It was a film about empire, emigration, longing and resignation. Each of the women talked about their families, their hopes and their disappointments, and I filmed them at work, at home and around the island.

It began to seem as if *Strangers* unknowingly fell into a number of filmic documentary categories. Was I making an 'actuality'? In fact, much of the footage was staged, to the point of one of the women dancing for the camera. The film was planned and structured and I did more than record what was before me.

Sharon R. Sherman points out, 'The reconstruction of the past was one of the prime motivators for studying folklore at the inception of the discipline.'[5]

Was *Strangers* a 'reconstruction of the past'? As another of the women talked about her childhood and events that had led her not to leave the country, I allowed that narrative to be explored filmically, dreamlike, by filming her behind a mosquito net, on her bed, but I was dealing with the present. My work explores the present by referring to the past. Migration was happening in all directions and I was curious as to why. Russell explains:

> Before World War II, ethnographic filmmakers were travelers, adventurers, and scientific missionaries intent on documenting the last traces of vanishing cultures.[6]

It seemed the tradition I was slipping into was one of the ethnographic film-maker. I was a traveller of sorts, a timid adventurer, and although Antigua was not known as a 'vanishing culture', the women I had first intended to film, a particular group of factory workers, turned out to be transient and by the time I arrived they had been deported and that particular part of the culture disappeared. I have never returned, so the culture did vanish for me, particularly as the following year a devastating hurricane demolished large parts of the island, further implying a vanishing. The ephemeral nature of life is one of the elements that film, and particularly documentary film, attempts to represent. Ethnographers have had a tendency to try to 'rescue "authenticity" out of destructive historical change.'[7] I was not attempting to fix or freeze the lives of the women in Antigua. The film explored how fear of the other in a small society mirrored the ongoing British anxieties about immigration. These women wanted change and improvements to their lives. On the island the fears of the indigenous population mirrored fears in Britain at that time.

Strangers

I became fascinated by the ever-changing definitions that the idea of documentary attracts. Fatimah Tobing Rony described the techniques deployed in this cinema as having three overlapping phases: the positivist mode of scientific research, the taxidermic mode canonized in *Nanook of the North*, 1922, and the commercial exploitation mode.[8]

At the time of making *Strangers* I was working with the local community in south London and aware of debates on race and identity.[9] I was an animator, used to working with the moving image and drawing. Making a documentary was a new direction for me. I was in Antigua for two months and worked with women factory workers. As an artist on the island, I was neither taking a 'positivist mode of scientific research', nor intentionally developing any sort of 'taxidermic mode'. However, the film has a certain 'preserved' feel to it. 'Commercial exploitation' was an unlikely outcome. I had made some enquiries for further sponsorship from television companies, but interest was not forthcoming.

Shortly after I made this film in 1988, I became aware of other modes developed from the modes espoused by Nichols. Having become aware of the categorization process, I discovered that categories continue to change and develop as time goes by and they tend to build on each other, as Sharon R. Sherman describes,

> Film theorist Bill Nichols has identified five modes used in documentary film for structuring its representation of events: expository, observational, interactive, reflexive (1991:33–75) and performative (1994:95). Each is created out of a dialectic with an earlier mode which has come to be conventionalized and stale. The changes occur historically, but each mode remains, affecting the others – either as a mode to be reacted against or as one to be incorporated in a new manner.[10]

More recently, in 2001, Nichols himself has described *six* modes of representation; 'poetic, expository, participatory, observational, reflexive [and] performative'.[11] When I reassessed *Strangers* according to these, it became clear that the mode I had used intuitively was predominantly 'allusiveness', as described by Peter Loizos,[12] where explanation is rejected, and the intention is to evoke thoughts in sounds and images. This was nearest to what I was attempting. *Strangers* was a story of internal or psychological journeys as well as of migrations to other countries. Choosing the 'poetic' definition explained my emphasis on 'the ways in which the filmmaker's voice gives fragments of the historical world a formal, aesthetic integrity peculiar to the film itself.'[13] I was using *Strangers* to evince some of the problems in wanting to move from the homeland, and used imagery of streets in Antigua as well as the Union Jack flag strewn Mall in London. The women revealed their stories in internal spaces, houses and workplaces, and the larger picture was reflected in use of external space, the airport, the sea and the forest.

Choice; power of choosing

The film attempted a compromise between aesthetic formal beauty and social comment.

Working outside a conscious awareness of documentary modes, my previous work had been a mixture of fantasy, animation and drama, so I was relieved to come across the work of Julia Lesage. She approaches her definitions from a feminist position and her clarifications meant more to me and allowed me to position the work differently. I particularly felt her emphasis on feminist experimental video autobiographies was significant. Even though *Strangers* was not autobiographical, her themes still resonated. She suggests four ways of classifying that relates to 'the video production process'. Reading the descriptions of these types of approaches made me consider some of my other films anew. In these I felt I was responding to the prevalent ideas of the time — psychoanalysis, gender politics, class, race and uses of the media. I had used animation, drama and installation work experimentally but now with hindsight I could reassess them.

Lesage asserts that existing information or data is the inspirational factor in the first type of autobiographical video. *Influence* (1983) was about a struggle, a psychological struggle with my mother. It was animated and used diary notes read aloud as the soundtrack. I was examining family patterns, the need to create and the battle for survival. In Lesage's description of this type of film there is usually voice-over, there is a certainty that key texts and material are available for use and related research is often incorporated. I began to feel I was a textbook case in making *Influence*. There were diaries from my past, material readily available to me, and 'the image track serves primarily to illustrate the verbal narration'.[14] At the time there was a new awareness of the personal being political, and bringing the more hidden areas of life into a public view felt confrontational.

Lesage's second definition includes works which 'contain internal evidence that they were made with a passion for the present moment'.[15] *Orkney Idyll* (1985) was in response to a holiday at midsummer on the Orkney Isles. The film is a celebratory record of a calm, peaceful place. Cows amble up to the camera, the sea laps onto the shore, the sky is intensely blue. It was a home movie and I have never made anything like it since. Passion for the present moment could be seen in *Cut* (1994), a short film made as a rapid response to Lorena Bobbitt cutting off John Wayne Bobbitt's penis. This was a news item in June 1993. I made the film in the following weeks, when news reports became obsessed with the event. I used animation of knives and scissors and an actress in a reconstruction of Lorena's preparations on a carrot. The soundtrack was readings from newspaper reports of the time, as well as a variety of cutting and snipping sounds. When shown at festivals, there was an enthusiastic response from the female section of the audience.

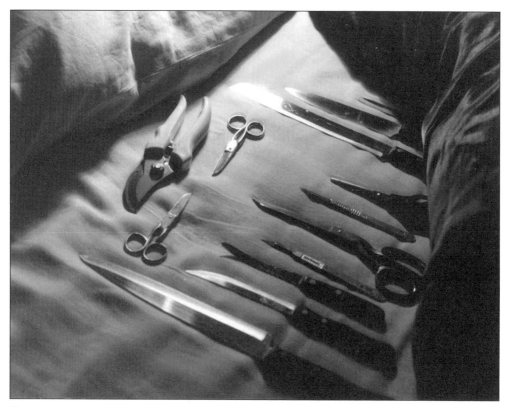

Cut

Lesage's third category, into which *Cut* could also fit, is called 'autobiographical fiction' where 'the maker moves from behind the camera and becomes a director of videography and actors at the same time'.[16] Usually there is a written script and the sound and image are structured and rehearsed. My short film *Choice, power of choosing*, which was made before Margaret Thatcher's use of the word 'choice' repositioned its meaning on the political right, was based on family events that happened a generation previously but which had an impact in the present. The film, recorded on Super 8, as well as using Hi-band Umatic, included my grandmother's voice-over of events in her childhood and a young woman acting her part. I had considered it a drama, now not only Lesage, but also Nichols, encouraged me to reconsider. Before categorizing documentaries, Nichols states there are only two kinds of film, documentaries of wish-fulfilment or documentaries of social responsibility.[17] *Choice, power of choosing* seemed to fit the documentary of wish-fulfilment group. I was telling a story of events in the past of my family, based on imagined as well as real occurrences. Until then I had thought of it as a drama, now I could describe it differently.

Lesage describes a fourth type of experimental feminist approach to autobiography where electronic media and animation allow fragmentation and layering. My first work that fits this description is a short film called *Ghost of the Artist* (2001) as part of the 'emplacements' project in St Petersburg. Technological influences changed my art/documentary practice. *Ghost of the*

Ghost of the Artist

Artist was filmed in a factory space which was located in the suburbs in the Red Banner factory, a renowned building designed by the modernist architect Eric Mendelsohn. This was explicitly about isolation and the factory spaces reflecting that. It was exhibited in the factory foyer, projected on vests manufactured by the factory, hung on a washing line. The entire video was made on the factory premises, exploiting the portability and accessibility of electronic media. The position and presence of the artist was evident in the video from reflections in the numerous shiny and reflective surfaces of the building. The building held echoes of modernism and I hoped my film would reflect this by using form more consciously and resisting narrative strands, as the journey through the factory had its own logic. I found I was working more experimentally, both in how I was making the video and how I was considering showing it.

Lesage again seemed to say what I had been thinking,

> ....to work in experimental video means to inherit the legacy of modernism, delighting in playfulness and using the art medium itself as a tool of discovery.[18]

I find the definitions of experimental video are closely linked to 'experimental' art. As an artist all my work is experimental, exploring risk, trying new things and approaching problems as experiments with a range of solutions.

Time Flies

When filming in Mendelsohn's factory, I deliberately chose to focus on the building rather than the people. I am reminded of the Wilson twins talking about their preferences when filming, relating to spaces and the architecture of buildings rather that the people within them. I wanted viewers to feel and appreciate my relationship to the space, and to notice that the feelings tended towards melancholy. *Ghost of the Artist* represented isolation and individuality. The solitary artist is glimpsed through various reflective surfaces and drifts apparently aimlessly through the factory space. Outside of the camera's frame, the factory was busy, peopled not only by the workers but also by almost twenty artists milling around, trying to express themselves through their work. The artists, by working in an inspirational space, seemed to bring definitions of art and documentary closer. Many video projections of the weeks of preparation, the explorations of the site and the surrounding suburbs were shown by artists with little experience of video making as part of their practice as sculptors and photographers.

A year later, following on from *Ghost of the Artist* I made another installation at a factory in St Petersburg, collaborating with architect and artist Irina Golovanok. While no longer self-reflexive, the video, as part of an installation at the factory, explored the workspaces within the factory, the city and the relationship to time. *Time Flies* exploited the accessible portable technologies of video and the laptop by using a small camera and various effects in editing.

Golovanok's interest in buildings and the history of architecture was used as a metaphor for time passing. The screen was split horizontally into thirds in the video installation. The top section showed a compressed view of a bus journey out of the city, while the lower third showed the journey in reverse. These were taken from inside the moving bus. The centre section was created out of stills, changing every second, of clocks in public places or wristwatches on people. The 'landscape' shape of the image was reduced and compressed as was the journey time, from forty-five minutes to seven, creating a synchronicity between the shape and the duration of the journeys. The work was projected onto the front entrance of the factory from within, so it could be seen from the street. We were making a record of a journey both in time and place, using shapes and sequences in a formal way and blending Nichols' poetic mode and Lesage's experimental type of autobiography. The journey was a personal one and the people showing us their wristwatches and clocks were relating to us directly but the formality of the structure and the presentation as an installation offered alternatives to personal and subjective readings.

Russell is interested in the relationship between diary film-making and radical ethnography.

> And yet autobiography in film and video is rarely a source of truth and authenticity, but a dispersal of representation, subjectivity, experience and cultural history.[19]

The gap between the truth and the reality shown in *Time Flies* might lead to some definition within radical ethnography about St Petersburg or its people on the streets and at work, but the video was designed as an art installation, so interpreting it as documentary leaves me yet again trying to decide what is art and what is documentary. Is it intention that defines the piece?

I am more interested in claiming that art and documentary are close, and truth in art is a less contested area than in documentary. Art has a more playful relationship with truth than documentary, which could be said to have a 'spacial relationship to the real'.[20] Even before Magritte showed us a painting of a pipe and told us a painting of a pipe was not a pipe, art has been understood as no longer trustworthy, images constantly deceiving us. It is harder to give up that belief and trust in documentary. Every frame is a photograph, and photographs are still trusted more. The trouble seems to be linked to the word 'documentary'. Instantly the 'big' words – truth, reality – become attached to the idea of documentary making. Elements in documentaries, for example, less narrative-led plots, or soundtracks offering atmosphere rather than information, or even images chosen for beauty, seem closer to art and so test our preconceptions of documentary.

Some of the categories became useful to me in my redefinition as an artist who uses documentary form. I have been able to group my work that previously I had not seen as commonly themed and I noticed that the autobiographic thread was stronger than I had realized. When I began using moving image in my work, I considered it as another tool in the artist's panoply. I continue to draw. In contemporary practice video has the same instantaneous effect as drawing. I can use video as a sketchbook, developing ideas and moving closer to documentary, or use drawing as a continuing link to art. What matters is that work is made. The categories come later. What influence these categorizations will suggest to new projects remains to be seen, particularly in extending the definitions to installation work, an area that seems to encourage art and documentary to work well together.

Notes

1. Peillex, G., *Nineteenth Century Painting*, Weidenfeld and Nicolson 1964, p. 33.
2. Babbitts, J., *Stereographs and the Construction of a Visual Culture in the United States, Memory Bytes*, eds. Lauren Rabinovitz, Abraham Geil, Duke University Press 2004, p. 127.
3. Nichols, B., *Introduction to Documentary*, Indiana University Press 2001, p. 1.
4. Russell C., 'The Body as the Main Attraction' in *Experimental Ethnography The Work of Film in the Age of Video*, Duke University Press Durham and London, 1999, p. 51.
5. Sherman S. R., 'The Folkloric Film, Historic Reconstruction, Visions of Ourselves', *Documenting Ourselves; Film, Video and Culture*, University Press of Kentucky 1998, p. 74.
6. Russell C., ibid., pp. 11 – 12.
7. Clifford J., 'Of Other Peoples: beyond the "Salvage Paradigm"', *Discussions in Contemporary Culture*, ed. Foster H., Bay Press Seattle 1987, p. 121.
8. Tobing Rony, F., *The Third Eye: Race, Cinema and Ethnographic Spectacle*, Durham, N.C.: Duke University Press, 1996, p. 91.
9. The Institute of Contemporary Arts had a series of conferences, 'Identity' was the basis of the sixth ICA Document and contained articles by Homi Bhabha, Stuart Hall and Jacqueline Rose, among others. (ICA Documents 6; Identity The Real Me, editor Lisa Apppignanesi, ICA London 1987.)
10. Sherman S. R., ibid., p. 260.
11. Nichols B., ibid., p. 99.
12. Peter Loizos, the Forman Lecture, Manchester conference of the Royal Anthropological Institute, 1989.
13. Nichols B., ibid., p. 105.
14. Lesage, J., 'Women's Fragmented Consciousness', *Feminism and Documentary*, editors Waldman D. and Walker J., Visible Evidence, vol. 5, University of Minnesota Press 1999, p. 311.
15. Lesage, J., ibid., p. 311.
16. Lesage, J., ibid., p. 311.
17. Nichols B., ibid., p. 1.
18. Lesage, J., ibid., p. 311.
19. Russell, C., ibid., p. xv.
20. Corner, J., *The Art of Record; a critical introduction to documentary*, Manchester University Press, 1996, p. 10.

Viewing Spaces and Audiences

Gareth Evans (interlocutor), Nina Pope, Claudia Spinelli in conversation

This panel investigated the ways in which the reception of productions has changed, and included Gareth Evans, writer and editor of *Vertigo* magazine, as interlocutor; Nina Pope, who works with Karen Guthrie as a group called 'Somewhere' (www.somewhere.org.uk) and who has used the Web to reach audiences, has recently co-directed their first film, *Bata-ville* (2006); and Claudia Spinelli, from Switzerland, who was curator of *Reprocessing Realities* (www.reprocessingreality.ch) which brought film-makers and artists together to 'observe and comment on the life around them'.

GE

It gives me great pleasure to be here this afternoon to moderate this final session. It seems to me that truth and dare should be raised here: once we enter these new spaces or think about hybrid relationships between them, then the truth will be 'up for grabs'.

Galleries, the Web and the street: with new spaces come new audiences and ways of interpreting art and documentary.

NP

Bata-ville is the only film we have made. We come from a background of working with new media and new technology, and our projects have encompassed a mixture of live events on the Web, using models a bit like live broadcast. All of them look at the different ways we can re-examine narrative or tell stories.

Often there is a concern with our relationship to the audience at the centre of our work, and quite often they are involved within the projects as collaborators and as part of the work.

One of the motivations to make this film was that we wanted to take control over the bit which came after the live part of its creation. We had done a lot of live projects where we were frustrated by the small audiences and with the way that after the event, we were not able to

Bata-ville 'We are not afraid of the future'. Production Still John Podpadec

have much control over what had happened. So with *Bata-ville* the idea for the artwork was that we would take people on this journey. It is essentially a road movie, but we wanted to be able to show it to a broader audience. That was our main motivation for making it into a film. It premiered at Edinburgh this year in the documentary section. I am not sure you would call it a documentary, although we do not mind it being referred to as such. In a way, it is a document of an artwork: a document of a week spent with a group of people. Some of the themes of the film are regenerational. But it is not a documentary about Bata shoe company or about regeneration.

I was originally asked to make a piece of public artwork for East Tilbury, one of the places that the film was about, so the film started as public art commissioned by Thurrock Council. I proposed that with the small amount of money they had available for public art, we could make an installation in the village which was a travel agency, and people could come and see me as a live travel agent. That fulfilled their requirement for a public artwork, and then from that, about a year later, we went on to fund-raise, make the trip and then make the documentary about the trip.

GE

We are grounded in this final session by concrete realities: by the film *Bata-ville* and by Claudia Spinelli's exhibition 'Reprocessing Reality'. Nina, did making your film resolve any questions for you about the dynamic between the various spaces you operate within?

NP

This morning a lot of people were trying to define documentary, whereas I was going back through our projects, thinking, 'what if you took out one word from the title and put documentary in instead'. So one of our first pieces is called a hypertext journal and it was a kind of Web diary, but, of course, it could be called a 'hypertext documentary'. Another piece took the 'Canterbury Tales' as a starting point for a live event and people told tales from different places. Again, if you replace '29 Tales' with '29 Documentaries', you see a natural progression towards making something in this way.

We are about to make another film so I guess that answers the question. We found ourselves very happy and at home with making and resolving work in this way, and once we had done

Bata-ville

it we thought, 'why didn't we do this years ago?' A lot of it is to do with distribution. It is fantastic that someone can rent this from 'Love Film' and see it in their home. There is a big audience out there: a lot of people do not have access to the Internet or phones but all of them have a copy of the DVD and apparently all of them have found some way of watching it.

GE

Is the word 'documentary' a problem because it comes with very professional implications? Would a word like 'document' be more helpful?

NP

I would prefer that, but our work has also been called 'new media' and 'engaged practice'. I don't feel comfortable with any of these terms. Yes, I would rather call it a document of the trip rather than a documentary, but I do not know if that will change over time.

GE

You said in your introduction that this was not about regeneration. Nor does it have a particular agenda in mind, but clearly as a result of making it, your own perceptions, as well as those of your passengers will change. Do you feel that making it has given you a statement?

NP

Maybe not a statement, but one of our aims was to put East Tilbury and Merryport, where the two UK factories are, in touch. We also went to Zlin in the Czech Republic, where Bata

TV Swansong artists: *TV Swansong - A Somewhere project - webcast 20/03/02*

originated. As the film gains a wider distribution, hopefully it will succeed in putting East Tilbury and Merryport on the map, as well as their recent industrial history. Merryport has a heritage agenda and is known for its Roman maritime history, but it does not include Bata and East Tilbury. This project was about asking people who came on the trip to think about the future, and what regeneration means to them.

GE

This idea of two dynamics, of the public and the private operating within the story that you followed and narratives that you created, is useful. You have a very public story that is centred in a factory and community, but many private versions of that story from the members of the community involved. Similarly, we engage with the film in a public space if we go to a festival, or privately if we watch it on DVD. So there are different versions of reality both in presentation and content floating throughout any experience you have with the film. Were you keenly aware of the purely productive nature of those collisions, or were you also alert to the problems that would come out of that?

NP

There were three groups of people on the bus, one from East Tilbury, one from Merryport and a group called the 'others' who did not work for Bata, so we did, to a certain extent, set up a situation whereby possible conflict or interaction might happen between them. Everybody who came was aware of what they had signed up for. They had applied to come, so in a way they were in a contract with us. But they were very generous to allow us to film what took place. We

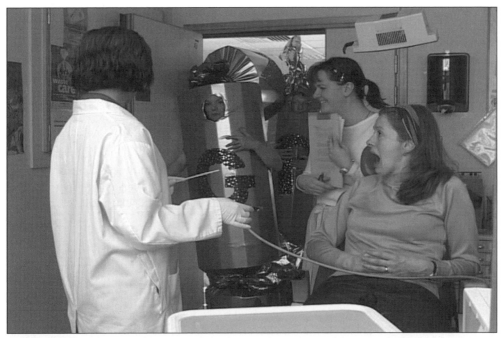

Pope and Guthrie's *Recommended Dose.*

had a video diary camera which a lot of people used on their own, despite being under no onus to do so.

GE

In terms of the contract to agree to expose oneself in one story in history it is very clear, but then in terms of how that is viewed by us in various locations, what were your thoughts about that shift in view?

NP

It is quite an intimate film. I was more able to anticipate how people might view it in their own home than I was able to imagine the experience of sitting at the back of the cinema with 200 people watching it. The first time we showed it was in East Tilbury and everyone in the village hall talked all the way through it because it was like watching their home video. Then we showed it at the Tate and people laughed in places we did not expect, or cried even. It was wonderful to be able to see the audience experiencing it, whereas when you broadcast something via the Web, you never get that intimate contact with a big group of people.

GE

There is the idea of this interface between spaces, but also this idea of how multiple truths co-exist within a single space. Claudia, could you say a little bit about how the recent exhibition you curated originated, in which a high-profile bank of artists were engaged in different senses of truth at the documentary/art/film interface?

CS

When I was asked to do that exhibition, I thought, 'Oh my God'. My main profession is an art critic and so I see a lot of exhibitions. I always find it problematic when you go to an exhibition with films that are long. Often you pop in the wrong moment, just in the middle of something, and so you miss the point and go out with bad feelings long before it ends. But then I began working and thinking about the issue. The solution I found was to put all emphasis on spatial and temporal dramaturgy. I took in a lot of installations, multi-perspective things that dealt with the physical presence within the real gallery space.

GE

You say, in the introduction to the catalogue, that the museum is not a place where we weep about the sad fate of unlucky people, but a context in which we can reflect on why something moves us, or why it leaves us cold. Was your initiative in setting this exhibition to investigate this?

CS

If you see the tradition of the exhibition space, the tradition of the museum, it is obvious that the meta-level is of great importance. I do not go to a museum to experience life, but to reflect about life. So even if I move physically in the space, it is always on this metaphoric level. Christoph Büchel, a Swiss artist in the exhibition, had a downloaded video from the Web for his work which showed a bomber plane destroying a village in Afghanistan. At first, it looks like a video game, but then you realize what you are looking at. So the emphasis shifts from pure information to questions of perception. The piece is not only about Afghanistan but also about the way your perception functions. Such a change of awareness is more apt to happen in the museum space than in its original context.

GE

In terms of the exhibition, what would the implications of it be for you as a critic? You are writing about working in diverse arenas and you are now creating this network of images that exists in a book format and also in a moment in time in a gallery space. Did you come out of it thinking that these relationships between documentary and art were radically changed from when you initiated the project?

CS

No, not radically changed. I realize now how difficult the job was and I hoped that the critics who went to see it, would take their time to see it properly. There was one critic that did not read enough in my vision, so this was putting me in the same position as people I criticized. On the other hand you can never force people to understand what you want to do: you just have to say, 'Here is what I can tell the world, take it or leave it.'

GE

We need to explore the multiple truths of the viewers and audiences. Could we put this into a production and an infrastructure context? Claudia was saying that she chose work ranging from the sculptural to the photographic with installation and single-screen image work. Perhaps it is true to say that if you are a film-maker in this country it is hard to be experimental. If you call yourself an artist, it might be hard to find the money, but it is much more acceptable to challenge form and content. Nina, can we ask you about your experience of funding structures? Because of your hybrid work, you must know about these rigorous areas of application.

NP
Bata-ville is weird. It was funded by different sources including the Heritage Lottery Fund, the European Cultural Foundation and the Arts Council. It was a mixed bag of funding, none of which was for film, because we had never made a film before. The project almost started as a joke about spending the regeneration money on a free holiday. We weren't allowed to write 'free holiday' on a lot of the press releases.

GE
Claudia, can you discuss European funding structures? Is there a situation where these issues are much more open and all the boundaries are gone and you can be yourself and apply openly and widely?

CS
Switzerland is not part of the European Union. It is easier to get money for art projects than for any film project because film is expensive and it has always been very complicated, so I don't think the situation is that different.

Of course you have to know how to write an application. What you say in them may be critically and politically subversive, that's not a problem. My exhibition, Reprocessing Reality, for example, is travelling to New York to P.S.1 Contemporary Art Center and was part financed by Pro Helvetia, which is like the British Council. We wanted to find private sponsors too, but that was hard because it is not an affirmative prestige object but an exhibition asking questions.

People who are at home in the film world expect a different kind of financing than people from the art world. If an artist is really established in the gallery context, his or her work is mainly financed by selling to private collectors or to institutions. In the show, I had one person from a film context explaining that he was used to everything being financed, and as this was for an art context it was very annoying. Usually artists work for free when you organize an exhibition, and you pay them maybe a meal or the production of the concrete installation, but you do not pay them for thinking or writing.

Cahal McLaughlin
When we discussed the notion of installations and the architecture of space on the first day, someone used a phrase about the space itself becoming 'psychologized'. I wondered what experience you have through your exhibition 'Reprocessing Reality' in terms of feedback. How do people respond, as unlike most other exhibitions which tend to be one-off installations, you had an enormous number of single- and multi-screen exhibits in one exhibition? What was the response to that?

CS
I suppose most of the public didn't watch all the work or take in all the work with the same concentration. But that is OK because everybody is different. I remember being at the exhibition and seeing an elderly couple and they really took their time to take in every work and they

Yervant Gianikian & Angela Ricci Lucchi. *Frammenti Elettrici.* © courtesy the artists

Yervant Gianikian & Angela Ricci Lucchi. *Frammenti Elettrici.* © courtesy the artists

Yervant Gianikian & Angela Ricci Lucchi. *Frammenti Elettrici.* © courtesy the artists

came down to talk to the woman who was on the front desk and they were almost destroyed mentally. I did not say anything because I had a bad conscience. Maybe it's a question of generations – that people of a younger generation are more used to dealing quickly with contents and working out what is interesting or not. That is probably something you have to learn or get used to.

GE
Nina, do you see the Internet working alongside film more directly, or can it mesh with film to be mutually productive?

NP
I don't think anyone could watch 93 minutes of *Bata-ville* on a tiny screen on the Net, but a lot of people experienced *TV Swansong* via the webcast, and still can now through the archives. It depends on the content, but I would not prioritize one over the other. With *TV Swansong* a lot of the excitement was meant to be derived from the sense that you were all watching it at the same time even though it was happening in lots of different places. Everybody knew that was the way people were going to watch the work, so they had that in mind when they were shooting it and when they were dealing with the sound etc. I've downloaded films to watch off the Web, but I have not watched them streaming.

GE
On a more philosophical level, the Web offers a relationship between solitary experiences, and yet is simultaneously shared, as you explored in a number of your projects. With this idea of a

Nyon: Philipp Gasser *I'm an Exhibition.* © courtesy the artist

community being created and made up of disparate individuals, does that inform the kind of work you would make?

NP

I am referring to *TV Swansong* a lot! Maybe I should have shown a clip of that. That whole project was about the demise of this shared, particularly UK-based, conversation around television. We don't really have the experience now where everyone watches the same warm, fuzzy programme at 7.30 on a Sunday evening. Instead, we can find other people who have the same shared interest as us, no matter how weird, and experience something with them. That is a significant shift in terms of who you are addressing through that work. That is what I was trying to hint at with this idea of having partial audiences for different pieces of work, or parts of the same piece of work.

One of our projects was a physical model of a text-based online game. So although you are dealing with people who are geographically dispersed, they have a particular interest and understanding of that part of the work, and you must address that, otherwise it is just a poor version of something that they can experience elsewhere. I don't think it works to distribute films only over the Web: it is about being targeted and specific and a lot of the films that are distributed in that way to tens of thousands of people, have a particular shared interest.

GE

Claudia, in terms of your own curation of the show, do you consider this idea of community when you are engaging with work as an exhibition programmer or as a writer? Do you think

Nyon: Guido Nussbaum *Heim-Welt II*. © courtesy the artist

that this idea of various communities that shift, ebb and flow around the work, affects your work?

CS
I think I can tell more concerning my writing. Where or for whom I write is of great importance. When I write for a news magazine, I imagine a public who is maybe interested, but does not know anything about art, a particular audience. Whereas when I write for an art magazine I write differently, relying on a specifically educated reader. Concerning the exhibition, I knew it was shown in a small town. Of course, part of the audience were the people from the film festival; I could imagine their approach whereas the concerns of the people who lived in that town were relatively unknown to me. Those were limits I had to accept.

GE
Elizabeth, how do you think this idea of the artist's work entering the documentary space works? You programme a wide range of documentary material at DocHouse, often sourced internationally. Have you a particular position on what it might mean to make or to show an artist documentary?

Elizabeth Wood, DocHouse
I am very interested in it. I did a series of lectures called *Across Borders* at Tate Modern, which brought artists and documentary makers together to discuss the area between them. It is interesting because we can all talk about funding artists' work, but really the issue is funding platforms for it to be viewed on, so I love to show artists' work as part of DocHouse. I show

Nyon: Reprocessing Reality. Installation View at Château de Nyon, April 2005. © courtesy gb agency, Paris & Postmasters Gallery, New York

international documentaries and there is something very special about getting together in a cinema with a documentary which has a certain energy about it. So I think that one of the most important things to lobby for is funding.

It is fascinating that FACT has actually done something about it in Liverpool. But in London there are very few places. Everybody here who is an artist wants to exhibit their work in one way or another. I would love to exhibit artists' work, but I have to pay the cinema to show the documentaries that I show, so I am unable to show multi-screen work. It would be excellent if there was a specific location. Unlike in the UK, European film-makers and artists make documentaries if they feel it is appropriate. I encourage you to see what the rest of the world is doing.

GE
Elizabeth Wood mentioned film-makers and I would be very keen to hear from artists, film-makers, practitioners, or whatever you like to call yourselves, about some of these experiences you might have had in relation to viewing spaces, to distribution or to exhibition. It would be great to get some concrete examples of what people have found in their own travels through the London-based, and international, arena. Are there any film-makers or artists here who would like to share some of their experiences about the themes in question?

Jini Rawlings, University of Westminster and artist
It is vital to get your work shown and seen. It was important to have a curator that actually saw my work and then supported me when I was making funding applications (almost rewriting the

funding application in some 'Arts Council-ese'), which meant that I then got other funding and a Leverhulme Artist-in-Residence.

I have a show on at the National Maritime Museum and had the Leverhulme grant which I used to buy two projectors. Claudia was saying film-makers expect to be paid. As artists, maybe we do not expect to be paid as much, but I think it is quite important that we do think about that.

GE
I would like to ask Claudia for a final summation of this particular session. What all these questions and issues throw up is the idea of work never settling into a single fixed form as it travels across spaces. Does this have significant implications for a contained piece of work?

CS
The intention of the artist is important. Of course you can encourage artists to try out something new, like the installation we had from Gianikian and Ricci Lucchi. It was not their own wish to project four films simultaneously, but the idea of Mark Nash, who collaborated with them as a curator. And, of course, such decisions make a difference. They influence reception and define a specific context which is part of the work and will influence its meaning.

GE
You engage directly with the world and there is always that open-ended relationship you have with individuals and communities and spaces. Does the idea of something constantly in flux attract you?

NP
It does attract me for some pieces, although the idea of having a DVD that I can give to people is attractive too. We were really shocked about how long the afterlife of making a film is. We made work before which was deliberately live – for example, the text-based game that goes on indefinitely or until the server breaks. *Bata-ville* is about to be sub-titled in Czech and English for yet another new audience, and we were horrified by the amount of time that takes.

GE
We live in an international city and receive images from all over the world. All these different film agencies and operations feed into the multiple truths of the image that we have been investigating during this conference. It has been very useful to bring some of these spaces into consideration, and so please do join me in thanking the panel for their contributions.

Vietnam/USA

Trinh T. Minh-ha in an interview by Eva Hohenberger

(This interview was first published in Germany – Verena Teissl/Volker Kull (eds.): Poeten, Chronisten, Rebellen. Internationale DokumentarfilmemacherInnen im Porträt. Marburg: Schüren Verlag 2006, pp. 294–308.)

Prologue

Hohenberger

You started filming as an amateur, after studying comparative literature and music, and after living in Senegal for some years. Could you talk a little bit about your beginnings as a film-maker? How did you get involved and how do you conceive of the status of the 'amateur'?

Trinh

I don't really see myself as an amateur, nor do I have any affinity with the 'professional' and the normative claims that accompany such an identification. These terms have very little relevance in my context, although I appreciate the way certain thinkers, like Barthes or Deren, redefined the amateur as an independent, 'counter-bourgeois artist' through their practices. I'm thinking here of the link drawn with *amator*, the one who loves, and hence of the emphasis put on pleasure and raw substance rather than on competition and conventional mastery. Film-making is certainly a work of love for me, so are writing and composing music.

I never thought I would be a film-maker. It happened quite accidentally in 1980, when I just returned to the States from three years of research and teaching music in Senegal. I was undergoing cultural shock, having moved from a vibrant, collective lifestyle in Dakar to the rather dull, isolated and highly individualistic context of academic life in Norman, Oklahoma. There were many reasons for making the difficult decision to leave Senegal, especially with regards to the educational system, which had been inherited from the old, pre-68 French system. But as with every loss, there's a gain. It was during that most depressive period of change that I began my activities as a film-maker. I befriended a number of artists teaching at the university there, and was introduced to the crafts of film-making through the generous exchanges I had with the film-maker Debbie Meehan. She now teaches in New York. It was thanks to her and to her assistant, Charlie Woodman, that I learnt film-making, literally from A to Z, and independently from the mercantile demands of the film industry.

EH

Your first films have been documentaries (*Reassemblage; Naked Spaces – Living Is Round*), in the meantime you have made seven films, two of them fictional. How do you conceive of the relationship between the two genres? Are there some things, some issues, which interested you but couldn't be represented in a documentary? By what criteria do you choose?

T

A film is primarily a film. At best, genres can be viewed convivially as different processes of reality and multiple creative practices for freedom. But in the film world, they are often hardened into definite categories bound to the politics of production, exhibition and distribution that determine the way people fund, consume and evaluate cinema. They set up hierarchical divisions aimed at reiterating prevailing power relationships.

For me, the best documentaries are those that remain aware of their fictional nature as image, and the best fictions are those that document the reality of their own fictions. People often ask whether my making feature narratives is indicative of a shift in my itinerary as a film-maker, because they tend to think that we can only work in one category. But the one luxury that independent film-making offers us is precisely the ability to shuttle – not necessarily from one category to another, but *between* categories. Whether the result leans more on the documentary or on the fictional side depends largely on the subject and the creative process.

In my practice, for example, 'documentary' may refer to an outside-in movement, where images are created by letting the world come to us with every move. And 'fiction' may refer to an inside-out movement, in which images are produced by reaching out to the world from the inside. These movements easily overlap in the between realm. If the materials recorded dictate the form the film will take, the subject of exploration designates which process would be most adequate for its unfolding.

EH

Besides filming you have also written extensively and all of your work, be it written or filmed, very strongly resists a clear assignment to a certain generic category. You always emphasize the space 'in between' or, concerning your way of working, 'the jump into the void', which means a kind of productive space that opens up new possibilities beyond the narrowness of certain aesthetic categories. But even if your work constantly crosses generic boundaries, such boundaries are nonetheless a necessary precondition for recognizing that you always try to transcend them. Only by knowing that there is such a category as 'documentary', will saying – as you did – that 'there is no such thing as documentary' make sense. Isn't that a constant paradox in your work, that it must necessarily presuppose boundaries to be able to work on their crossings?

T

Your raising this question and gearing our conversation toward the documentary is largely due to our context of production – to the fact that this interview is meant for a book on documentary film-makers. So the question performs that very paradox it is pointing to and tells us something about the conditions for paradoxes.

It's important not to confuse the film with the discussion around it or with the theoretical work that comes with it. What the experience of film offers cannot be duplicated or explained verbally. This is why, as said in *Reassemblage*, 'I do not speak about' but only 'nearby'. This applies to the nature of the commentary or the aphorisms in the film as well as to my own practice as I speak and write. I theorize *with* my films, not *about* them. The relationship between the verbal, the musical and the visual, just like the relationship between theory and practice is not one of illustration, description or explication. It can be one of inquiry, displacement and expansive enrichment. The verbal forms a parallel track and is another creative dimension.

In public debates and in interviews, the terms of the discussion are initially determined by concerns of viewers that are not necessarily the initial concerns of the film-maker. My intentions and motivations are only part of what goes into the readings and theories advanced, which are also built on the unpredicted interactions among elements in the work, and are often densely populated by other people's feedback. Boundaries come primarily with viewers' expectations and one addresses them as one learns of them. Rather than being the preconditions for any creative work, they are pseudo-problems that arise with our limits in reception. As I've specified elsewhere, my films are not made in reaction to anything; this is not enough to motivate me to create. They are made because of a number of strong encounters and feelings such as the love that one has for one's subjects of inquiry, for example.

It may help to read the quote you made in context. I wrote: 'There is no such thing as documentary...despite the very visible existence of a documentary tradition.' The paradox is here fully acknowledged; it is part of the provocation issued to draw people's attention to the documentary establishment's misleading claims. On the one hand, anyone working intimately with the reality and the materiality of film would feel at odds with categories that merely reflect the way society compartmentalizes knowledge into 'expertise' for the purposes of control and consumption. When assumed, the place of paradoxes, which exceeds reaction and opposition, can be a very lively place. On the other hand, there are many ways to enter my films: with or without baggage; through the plastic, the theoretical, the political or several dimensions at once. There is something for every viewer, and those who enter them freshly, sensually in now-time without always trying to make sense, usually get a lot out of them. This has little to do with any knowledge of film traditions.

The Aesthetics of Documentary

EH

After seeing your last film, *Night Passage*, it seems a little strange to address you as a documentary film-maker. The film tells the story of a girl who becomes adult by overcoming severe experiences of loss — she has lost her mother and her best friend — in a way, through aesthetic experiences. In a certain sense one could say that this is a canonical story in which the topic of a journey is read in a psychological way; travelling becomes exploring the yet unknown self by exposing oneself to yet unknown experiences. But what is striking is that the journey may also be seen as a kind of time travel through the history of artistic media, or better,

Night Passage Denice Lee

through the aesthetic use of media – aesthetic in the very basic sense of perception. Kyra, the main figure, is given opportunity to perceive, one might even say the 'healing' force of aesthetic experience which is strongly tied to the body. Her commitment to the art forms presented is not just watching as usually encountered in cinema, and seeing is always related to a bodily sensation or action. For example, there is a wonderful scene where she experiences sounds together with taste or another one where she and her friends experiment with colours making sounds depending on how they move on the coloured surfaces. The film might be seen as a strong argument for the synaesthetic pleasures offered by all kinds of aesthetic media production. I see here a link to your documentaries because they work with similar principles of synaesthetic pleasure. Can we take *Night Passage* as a statement about your aesthetic commitment and position aside from the boundaries between genres? Would you say that there is a specific aesthetic position in your work and how would you yourself describe it?

T
There are many ways to name this commitment. I would say that my films are made to shift our perception of reality and experience of cinema – which involves the whole of our body. This is aesthetics' radical force. When reality starts speaking to us differently, one can easily 'get high' with aesthetics as it leads to what I've called 'an elsewhere within here'. Indeed, without an awareness of its social and existential dimension, aesthetics remains largely conventional and normative.

The politics of form, which includes but is not reduced to the politics of representation, may be said to be a constant in my work. So is the spirit of witnessing that runs through the films,

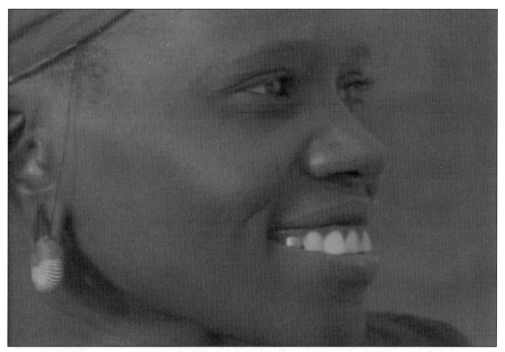

Reassemblage

cutting across genres and categories. It is very adequate to take *Night Passage* as a point of departure for discussing my aesthetic position, but as with every film I've made, the commitment is always at least twofold – two, not merely as a duality, but as a radical shifter that designates many twos or a multiplicity. Structuring artistic principles can be perceived simultaneously in their plastic and cinematic effects and in their social implications. Every statement advanced in the film can be understood within its story space or in the gap between screen and spectator, as a reflexive device and a witnessing voice. The matter is the form. By committing to form one commits to content and vice versa. As with my previous films, which offer multilevelled perception and reception, *Night Passage* is made to function on more than one level of reality. And while all levels are interactively related, each runs independently with its own rules and logic.

The time-space in which the different materials of the cinematic fabric – images, graphics, words, music and environmental sounds – are woven, is that of a multiplicity. Their expansive relation in my films is not one of domination and subordination. Ear and eye, for example, never duplicate one another. They interact in counterpoints, syncopations, offbeats, and polyrhythms – to borrow some musical terms. Rhythm is the base from which form is created and undone. It determines both social and sensual relationships. In the play of hear and see, silence and sound, stillness and movement, many viewers have vocally remarked that images in my films make them hear while the soundtrack makes them see. The hearing eye and the speaking ear are constantly at play, and form is arrived at only to address the formless. These are the two facets of a single process – or of life and death.

Surname Viet Given Name Nam

EH

Even if *Night Passage* is a fiction film there are some documentary parts in it. All the artists Kyra meets seem to play themselves and while representing figures of the fictional world they perform their arts as they would do on stage. Some of them even give statements about their work like the sculptor. So in a certain sense one might call the film at least partly a documentary about some individual artists. On the other hand the topic of doubling seems very prominent in the film: Kyra and her friend often watch scenes which double their lives; the two girls double each other like the female dancers double the girls; there are two storytellers and even the fathers of the girls seem to double each other. In the prominence of the motif one might see a reworking of the problem of identity, but also a statement about the ontological nature of photographic arts which double the object/person before the camera. When you speak about the 'witnessing spirit' of the film, is there any connection here between 'to witness' and 'to double'?

T

What a great coupling. Your comment on doubling in relation to the issue of identity and the nature of photographic art is absolutely right on the mark. I have elaborated elsewhere about alterity being radical to the definition of an image. My image is there where I am not, literally and physically speaking. The encounter with one's otherness and the spectral me can be very disturbing. Some of my psychoanalyst friends are, for example, very sensitive to mirrors in a room. As I happen to have plenty of them at home for *Feng-shui* purposes (the science of living with the environment), when these friends come to visit me, they scrupulously turn their backs to the mirrors.

Naked Spaces – Living is Round

In art across cultures, representations in doubles of divinities, or plants and animals, for example, refer to the double aspect of every life force: the yin-yang of existence or the positive-negative of things, both in terms of social values and of photographic imaging. As in a process of sedimentation, the self's geological layers can unexpectedly show its ancient colours when the many buried me's surface into the conscious me through small and big incidences. The double in the domain of self-knowledge is quite common; so is the reading of the encounter with one's double as a sinister event. To see one's double is to see oneself dead.

In their night passage, most of the encounters Kyra and Nabi have as they enter darkness upon leaving the train are those likely to open a window into their true nature (as with Kyra in her identity struggle) and to invite them gradually, in diverse exposures, to get 'in the water', so to speak. Here, the water that kills is also the water at the source of beings. Echoes, twins, mirrors, couples and doubles abound in the film. The two young women's voyage is strewn with echoing words, laughter and sounds; with digital images that mirror and repeat ad infinitum in immortality; and with enlaced bodies that struggle in the dances of fire and water.

In fact, only the beginning and the ending of the film refer to its fictional source of inspiration, which is a novel by Kenji Miyazawa. The rest, or the entire development of the film, remains ambivalent in its status, because the material shot is largely based on collaborative work and on performances improvised by the artists involved: the sculptor; the robot-designer-philosopher; the musicians on screen (drummers and electronic composers); the cyberscientist and technicians; the many fire performers, masked dancers and twin dancers who move in pairs.

Shoot for the Contents

This constitutes the documentary part of the film, which focuses not so much on the individual artists *per se* as on their practices of art as means of transformation.

Witnessing as a guiding spirit of the film is not only to be found in the main characters' roles in the encounters they make, it is also very explicit in the way the camera refuses to enter the realm of psychological realism by consistently looking at and from the exterior. There is no attempt to 'get inside the characters' or what they express. Witnessing, not merely as grasping something on the run as in news coverage, but as a relation to the self in which the indefinite doubling and multiplying unsettles any sense of fixed identity. In short, witnessing as a state of being: the open ear and eye that let things come on their own accord and at their own pace.

EH
I would like to talk about another scene in *Night Passage* which I liked very much and which seems to point to certain problems of documentary as well. It is the scene where the two girls meet the (female) scientist: She starts talking by reading a definition of an animal, then asks the two girls to help her hang filing cards on a clothing line. She then talks about language itself, thereby literally losing her head (her head goes out of focus). For me this scene formulates a funny and self-ironic statement about scientific work that after all forms part of your own work. Starting with the desire to get a hold of things by naming them correctly and having the statement written down, science ends up with the ambiguities of language itself; if language can't catch the world, how could images? And what could this mean for documentary which for Bill Nichols belongs to the same 'discourse of sobriety' as science?

T
Yes, well said, for language, like the image, is fictional by nature. Scientific findings can be far more 'incredible' than religious beliefs or outer space imagination. For me, the most moving and challenging works in the sciences are those that remain aware of the inevitable role of fiction in furthering experiments. Science needs poetry, and no scientific description can be separated from its mode of observation. The performative and self-reflexive scope of the scene you mention extends to the entirety of the film.

A Tale of Love

The scene also features the web of endless words in which we fare as 'the sound people make...that can be caught hold of since each person has a different vibe'. With new technology, as remarked by the woman researcher, 'sound prints are like fingerprints and soon, we'll exist digitally, we'll be able to hear sermons and lectures made a thousand years ago'. The obsessive desire to preserve, to record and to archive for the purposes of memory plays a large role in the making of documentary. Collecting data, objects and information for information's sake partakes in the 'museumification' of things and events. What seems indispensable to a dominant mode of knowing appears recklessly ignorant to other modes of living. For, remembering in the context of a museum display, archival classification, history retrieval and reality documentation go hand in hand with the process of profound forgetting. Of relevance here, for example, is the struggle of Native Americans to reclaim the bones of their ancestors – and with these, *history* in their own words. Such a fight goes to the heart of power relations. It calls for the necessity to move beyond material cause and evidence to restore agency to the marginalized in an exploitative system of visibility.

Documentary is often equated with truth, and narrative fiction, with imagination. But as it is well known, reality is often stranger than fiction. It is far more fascinating than what we can come up with, for the 'real' cannot be reduced to the visible, the tangible or the material. Fact is not truth. Accumulating facts does not necessarily lead to truth, and just as one gathers them to prove, one can also use them to falsify, negate or disprove. The politics of interpretation is always at work. What I question at length in my films are the factitious claim to objectivity and the pursuit of naturalism in the development of a media technology that promotes the illusion of increasingly unmediated access to reality.

EH

I would like to talk about language in your films, especially interviews. The device of the interview seems a good example; usually interviews belong to documentary where they fulfil a specific function: integrated in a chain of arguments they stand out as formulating a kind of truth which is independent from the one who argues. And it seems to be exactly this function which you try to explore in many of your films, whether one calls them documentary or fiction. The question always seems to be what it means to speak in front of a camera. It is interesting to note that in your documentaries you try to avoid any naive speaking of a protagonist. Rather than using 'normal interviews' you prefer creating a kind of experimental setting like in *Surname Viet* or *Shoot for the Contents*, or you do without interviews at all like in *Naked Spaces* and *The Fourth Dimension*. Is the 'normal interview' too worn out in your eyes? Or do you avoid it because of its implicit power relations?

T

I did call the interview 'an antiquated device of documentary' in *Surname Viet*, where the politics of interviewing and of subtitling as well as the question of language and of translation in self-representation are structurally featured. But as you've noticed, although I may not use them in certain films, interviews are an important part of my work, both in film and in book forms. Addressing the politics of form requires innovative imagination, for each film is a new challenge of the 'how', 'what', 'when' and 'where'. Thereby, exposing the workings of the interview is not a mere question of avoiding 'normal interviews'.

As you can tell by our interview and by those published in *Framer Framed* and *Cinema Interval*, one of the constant 'abnormalities' is that I don't just answer questions, because it's the 'inter' in interviews that appeals to me. The encounter between us is an encounter not between ready-made sound bites, but between languages, cultures, concepts, events and processes. It offers a third ground from which I work at shifting the nature of the points raised, using them as departures to offer an expansive field of practice in film-making. This takes time and space on the page; it raises problems of choices and limits as related to the number of characters we're allowed for publication.

Power relations lay at the core of normative representations. I've previously spoken at length on the deceptive mechanism of questions and answers and on the problematics of 'giving voice' in the positioning of interviewer and interviewees. What I find refreshing is your take on it — that it all boils down to the issue of speaking in front of a camera. This is where documentary and fiction, or witnessing and acting, meet on the film screen.

EH

The interview is only one of the dominant modes of speaking in documentary, the other is the commentary. It may assume a broad variety of language forms, from a subjective poetic language to a factual, technical one. In what is called auteurism in documentary we often find the commentary to be the most prominent place for the film-maker to inscribe herself in the texture of her film. Conversely, the audience learns to distinguish voices and ways of speaking, the professional voice from the voice of the amateur. The latter can function as a door opener that helps the viewer/listener to get involved in a situation where he/she feels to be addressed personally. You have always used commentary very sparingly. In *Naked Spaces* the commentary consists of a montage of quotations by very different authors and people and you had it spoken by three female voices, including your own. When you spoke by yourself in *The Fourth Dimension* it was immediately noticed and mentioned in almost every review of the film. Why have you been so cautious with your voice?

T

Your question seems to raise two issues: that of the commentary in general and that of my voice, more specifically. I've touched on the first one earlier when I discuss the relation between music, image and text in my film, in which the verbal is treated not as a comment about the image, that is, as an instrument to give meaning to the visual, but as a creative element of its own. In our need to come up with meanings and to impose them, we tend to use and consume language in its most reductive function. But language has its own complexity and multiplicity, which can offer a very fertile ground for artistic realizations. On the one hand, meaning is a mental construct; it's just *one* dimension of language. On the other hand, the poetic force of a commentary, a physical voice or a tonality has little to do with what people commonly view as 'poetry'. You don't need to write a poem or to rhyme verses in order to produce poetry, which is not only aesthetic, but also social and existential — a state of being.

Similarly, speaking through my voice in the first person 'I' is not necessarily personal or subjective, at least not in the way these terms are usually understood. For, I'm not trying to get at any internal essence, and my films do not lead to self-interiority as with psychological realism. On the contrary, working at ceaselessly undoing preconceived images, sounds and words and, hence, at freeing the film from any single authoritative centre, not only 'I feel less and less the need to express myself', as stated in *Reassemblage*, but also I respect the opacity effect of the unknown other.

However, where being cautious may help is when objectivity is claimed in 'giving voice'. Documentaries often fall prey to the ideology of transparent representation. They naively pretend to be neutral in presenting the two sides of things through pros and cons. But what tries to pass for objectivity is often no more than a non-committed stance unaware of its own politics. In affirming righteously that one opens a space for those who do not have a voice, one often forgets that the gaining of voice happens within a framed context, and one tends to turn a blind eye to one's privilege position as 'giver' and framer — albeit a framer ultimately framed as well. Exposing this very power relation through subtle cinematic devices that make the viewer surreptitiously aware of the film-maker's position remains a real challenge with each new work.

EH

Another device you constantly explore seems to be lighting. The whole tradition of direct cinema and its ideological implications, first of all the inseparable bond between technology and immediacy, put the device of lighting on the side of fiction film. For documentary there exists an ideology of 'naturalness' which tries to make invisible all technology that is necessarily part of the film-making process, and lighting was one of the first 'sacrifices' of this ideology. In your films lighting gains back an important place and role, you even work together with Jean-Paul Bourdier who is credited for 'lighting design'. The word 'design' alone points to a non-spontaneous way of working, thus leading the work in the direction of fiction. Beyond the claim for visibility, which for most documentaries seems to be the sole intention for lighting, what parameters govern your concept of lighting?

T

When I am doing the cinematography myself, lighting is conceived quite intuitively. I have always disliked clinical images, by which I mean the kind in which lighting is used only to make the object of focus legible to the viewer. It's all linked to the way one relates to what is being filmed. Instead of 'going at it', and treating it as an object to be captured, the camera can look at the filmed subject non-possessively, sliding on its surfaces, passing nearby and caressing it, for example. So the lighting comes from this kind of attitude: how do you light a subject if you don't want to simply present an object? What you come up with would be based on your own rapport to your subject and on your attitude in relationships.

When I have to direct and therefore to work with a cinematographer as in the interviews scenes of *Surname Viet Given Name Nam* and *Shoot for the Contents*, or as in the fiction films, *A Tale of Love* and *Night Passage*, I rely on Jean-Paul's talent as an architect and designer. Lighting is then treated the way language and music are treated in the relation between ear and eye – that is, as a creative dimension and a visual 'track' in its own right. Its function is not to serve actors and their environments as in conventional narratives, nor does it hide itself in the pursuit of naturalism as in conventional documentaries. It has its own rules and logic in acting on the senses. These change with each film, but if I had to generalize, I would say that Jean-Paul's attitude to light and colour is radical: he has no affinities for the discreet charm of the bourgeois range of pastel colours. Lights come in primary colours and in distinct, punctual shapes. This is true for the films mentioned, except for *Surname Viet*, whose lighting stays closer to my two previous films shot in Africa in playing on the contrasting blue and orange spectrum of film colouring.

Exploring lighting as a cinematic gesture of its own here has very little to do with what the film world calls 'theatrical lighting'. I've discussed elsewhere the social connotation of primary colours in working with multiplicity and the racial colour line. The dance of colour is, in all senses of the term, a tale of humankind. Being 'colour blind' in our society should not simply be understood as being oblivious to colour, but rather as being blinded by the vanity of colour – the way discrimination based on skin colour is. 'The five colours will blind a man's sight', says a statement in *Shoot for the Contents*. It is with this critical perspective that we work explicitly with colours, all the while disliking the chatter of visible things. Visibility is not our main concern, and our cinematographer (Kathleen Beeler) has often had to remind us of the factor of legibility in the process of image-making.

Whenever there's a choice, we would prefer a contour in darkness rather than a full legible surface in functional or illustrative light. The quality of darkness determines the quality of light.

EH

Music also has always played an important role in your films; but while it is usual to have a score for fiction films, it is not usual to have a score for documentaries. Since *A Tale of Love* you have worked with a group called The Construction of Ruins. In *The Fourth Dimension* you show a lot of Japanese ceremonies with their original sounds, mostly flutes and drummers, but you also added a composition by The Construction. Can you tell about the process of weaving together the original and the composed sounds? And how did you integrate your commentary?

T
We can see it as a conversation among sounds. The process is no different than the ones I've discussed earlier concerning the use of words, images, rhythm and lighting. It's all a matter of multiplicity and independence in close relationship. The specific sound of an event, a location, a body or an object is woven, the way musical motifs and notes are, into the fabric of non-representational sound improvised by the musicians of The Construction of Ruins. Music and sound design is the part I enjoy the most in putting together the film. But, it is also the part most difficult to verbalize, because music is a dematerialized art, and one that easily frees itself from representation.

In mainstream film sound, the ear is subordinated to the eye; the visual track comes first and the soundtrack is there only to serve the image, illustrating it, giving it the realism it lacks and amplifying it when it fails to convince, for example. This is why a number of film-makers whose strength lies primarily in the image (like Sohrab Shahid Saless, Andrei Tarkovsky, Alexander Sokurov or Bela Tarr) tend to dismiss music and its superfluous, ornamental role in film. They avoid or minimize the musical in their works and use enhanced environmental sound for intensified psychic effects. But for me, the taken-for-granted divide between noise and music, which has been so important to the ear trained in western classical music is quite obsolete. Every sound, every so-called noise can be made musical, especially when one works intensely with rhythm, resonance and vibration. The soundtrack should in every way be as inventively powerful as the visual track.

The Ethics of Documentary

EH
Another question at the centre of your work is the question of representing 'the other'. I put 'the other' into quotation marks, because it conveys such a wide range of topics and subjects in your films. The other may be a cultural artefact like African architecture and music in *Naked Spaces*, a social group like the Vietnamese women living in the United States in *Surname Viet Given Name Nam*, a person like Kieu in *A Tale of Love* or a country we don't know much about like China in *Shoot for the Contents*. Defining the other as other may depend on anthropological assumptions (everybody or everything beyond myself is other to me, which implies for me, for example, certain ethical tasks) or it may depend on political power relations which are usually quantified by the idea of majority and minority. The other is always a relational concept, necessarily bound to an idea of identity on the one side, from which 'the other' differs. Seen from a more functional than anthropological perspective, one may perhaps say that every society, in reproducing itself at the same time produces the notion of otherness. In this (re)production it relies on political and juridical procedures as well as on symbolic or aesthetic ones. Each society has at its disposal a number of stereotypes in representing the other, may it be for negating its difference or for foregrounding it. Isn't it hard to escape these stereotypes because they are deeply rooted in the historical unconscious, as well as the idea of otherness

itself? How would you describe your concept of otherness and how is it possible to avoid falling into the traps of stereotyping the other in the process of representation?

T

This is not a subject I can summarize in a few lines, that's why I've written a whole book on it, *Woman, Native, Other*, in which I've had to use the entire range of personal pronouns to explore the radical relationship of self and other. A few examples of 'other' in my work and its politics of naming: the inappropriate/d — woman, native, handicapped, abnormal, deviant, queer, foreign, refugee, not-yet-citizen, non-aligned, marginalized, silenced, dominated, oppressed — in other words, all those who stray from the norms of man, mankind and human. And with these, the other within: the West in me, or the Master, the dominant I, the sovereign subject, the Us versus Them, the omniscient, rational outsider, and more — all also inside me.

Viewed both negatively and positively, and depending on one's attitude in relationship or one's positioning in specific situations, the other is the one who escapes one's control and exceeds the self indefinitely. Power relations are of an infinitely complex nature, and this is a challenge I've had to take up with every work I undertake. Sometimes one cannot avoid falling into traps, but if one witnesses the falling and the setting of traps, then one can use stereotypes for what they are, in order to undo them and shift the terms of fixed representation.

EH

The question of otherness as well as the question of speech directly leads to ethical issues, which seem inseparable from the aesthetic ones. Ethical questions, one could say, are concerned with problems of responsibility. In your writings you develop some concepts which seem to cover both, aesthetic and ethical questions. One of these concepts is the concept of 'speaking nearby', which is opposed to the idea of 'speaking about' (something or someone). Usually documentaries speak about or, as in the case of the interview, delegate speech to someone else, who then speaks about. Could you explain the concept in this double perspective of ethics and aesthetics?

T

It's a very simple concept, and yet, when you haven't practised it, it may appear abstract or cryptic. In the context of power relations, speaking for, about, and on behalf of is very different from speaking with and nearby. To give an example from our everyday, if someone very close to you, like your lover or your mother is the subject of your discussion, how would you speak? If that person is not with you when you talk, then you can easily speak about her even though your close relationship already makes it uneasy for you to objectify her. But if she is right next to you, then you'll have to speak differently, being attentive in everything you say to the fact that she can talk back. Once you pay sustained attention to this, your ear becomes attuned to the way a person negotiates his or her space in producing intuitively a speech based on this awareness of power relations in knowledge. The very palpable lack or presence of such an intuitive grasp is what immediately strikes me in listening encounters.

Making a film that shows and speaks with the subject of your inquiry as if they are listening and looking next to you would shift subtly but radically your mode of address, of framing and contextualizing. Whether this subject is actually present or not, doesn't matter; you're committed to speaking nearby him, her or it. What has to be given up is first and foremost the voice of omniscient knowledge. Similarly, speaking nearby my films also implies, for example, that I can tell you what I do in these films – the thought and making processes that go into their realizations – but I cannot tell you what they mean or how to experience them. Meanings can always be expanded at infinity when one speaks nearby. In positioning your voice next to, you acknowledge that there's a space in-between, an interval of possibilities, and you learn to speak with audible holes and gaps. As in *Reassemblage* or in *Night Passage*, questions such as 'what is the film about?' and 'where are we going?' can only be answered anew each time with the cooperation of the viewer.

The Politics of Documentary

EH
Since its beginnings as a distinct film genre, documentary has been used for political reasons, to persuade people, to strengthen their beliefs in certain political values or to produce a certain image of their society. In this sense documentary has always served as a political instrument. After World War II, the educational, persuasive and propagandistic functions of documentary were taken over by television, which is a highly nationalized medium and which first and foremost serves national(istic) purposes. After the Civil Rights movements and their use of independent media, we have witnessed a repoliticalization of documentary rooted in an open conflict with television. This new 'movement' accuses television of lying and tries to establish itself in counterpoint, by telling the truth. Michael Moore's *Fahrenheit 9/11* may be an example. But insofar as this new political documentary remains deeply connected with television, it also shares television's ideology of truth. How can we conceive of political documentary in another way? Do we have to remember 'the lessons of Godard', for example, and his famous sentence that we shouldn't just make political films but film in a political way? And wouldn't that mean to follow up with some old avant-garde ideas such as the constructivist politics of form? Can these ideas still be valid and useful?

T
Nothing is more conventional than an approach to politics that is aimed at the most obvious location of power: the head of state and other personalities of the body politic. It's fast-food politics. Sometimes we take advantage of it, the way we may eat a McDonald hamburger on the run because it's fast and cheap, and allows us to partake in the illusion that it serves the average lower middle class. The reactive claim to truth and the open conflict with television has a role to play in these times of global fear officially maintained via pathological lies. But it is nothing new when we think of the pioneering work of Marshall McLuhan in the late 60s (*The Medium is the Message*). However, what seems 'new', for example, is the (Cannes) validation of this conflict at a time when the European and American superpowers are at odds with each other concerning the war in Iraq.

For me politics permeates our everyday, it is a dimension of one's consciousness in being. People talk about getting temporarily involved in it or about mellowing down and leaving it altogether at some stage of their lives. But politics arises in all of our activities, whether we recognize it or not. Godard's distinction between making a so-called political film and making films politically is here very adequate. It helps to widen the scope of the political, freeing it from the domain of economics and established institutions of power. The implied refocus on a calibre of consciousness in the making process or on form as inseparable from content serves as a reminder of how films about progressive actions can ultimately prove to be regressive in their unquestioned replication of structural relations of power.

Similarly, the politics of form cannot be reduced to the series of 'isms' that mark social and artistic movements. Form in its radical sense should address the formless; it ultimately refers to the processes of life and death. Affirming form is recognizing the important contribution of each vibrant life as a continual creative process. All the while, letting form go is acknowledging our own mortality — or the necessity to work with the limits of every instance of form. This is how the question of multiplicity and the politics of identity can be viewed at best. And this is also what I've been doing with every film and with *Night Passage*, which focuses on friendship and death as a response to a specific political moment of our time.

The Technologies of Documentary

EH

The Fourth Dimension was the first of your films to be shot with digital video, but instead of using this technology to increase the impression of authenticity the film points to quite a different direction. The new technology sometimes appears to be a tool to examine the older film technology. This impression is even stronger when watching *Night Passage*, where one of documentary's central metaphors, the window to the world, is constantly explored by foregrounding the function of the frame and the whole process of visibility/invisibility which is at play during a film's projection. You even deal with the whole history of visual media, starting from shadowgraphs and ending with digitally produced scientific images, with a very long sequence in the middle, where you expose the basic principle of cinema (light moving in time or light writing) in your technical treatment of a group of fire performers. Can you tell a bit about your way of using new technologies?

T

In turning to digital technology for the production of my last two films, I have been working more intensely with time — as referred to by the title *The Fourth Dimension*, and as dictated by the medium itself. I've also been working with what I call 'still speed' (in my book, *The Digital Film Event*) to characterize what this technology can offer and seems best at. Formed via a scanning mechanism, the digital image is continuously in the process of appearing and disappearing. Its inherent mutability doesn't really allow one, for example, to produce a still image, for movement continues, unfinished, in the 'freeze frame'. This can profoundly affect one's sense of time, one's yearning for immortality and one's response to death.

These are all the focuses of *Night Passage*, both thematically and structurally speaking. As with my previous works, this film turns around on itself and looks at itself in the act of coming into being. Such performative reflexivity, which throws the making and looking self into an abyss, is a way of exposing our limits and addressing our mortality. Digital systems are founded on binary structures of 0s and 1s. On off on off. Now 1. Now 0. The mercantile mind has not failed to appropriate this to economic ends and as the trend shows, narratives are now likely to come in sequels, the audiences being kept in wait for the next, more sensational episode yet to come. I deal with this ethics of disappearance and re-appearance quite differently. In *Night Passage*, where film and video aesthetics co-exist without one being subsumed to the other, the magic of digital technology may be seen subtly in the transitions for which I use the dissolve as a structural device — one that I have never resorted to in analogue film, preferring then the straight cut, or even the jumpcut.

Everything in *Night Passage* reflects and performs the notion of passage, and with it, the continual morphing, the state of transformation during the trajectory towards death, the fading into darkness, no form or the void, *and* the return anew on screen. What computers offer in cyberspace is so fascinating that we relish in the endless possibilities of special effects. We let our computers rule our lives, leaving them on all day, all night so we can access information at the speed of light through our fingertips. In this age of Augmented Reality and of Remote Control where relationships away from the computer are at stake, we may have to learn anew when to turn the machine on and when to turn it off.

EH

The notion of technology may not only point to the development and uses of hardware (technics) but following Foucault also to certain productive social procedures which imply technics but are embedded in other discursive mechanisms. Thus, one might talk about documentary (in Nichols' sense of a 'discourse of sobriety') as being a technology of truth. You have always been sceptical about the notion of truth, at least about the idea of a single one, but don't scepticism and relativism lead one to abandon the idea of truth altogether? Don't we need 'truth' as a kind of halt or stop sign beyond which would reign the powers of 'everything goes'? Shouldn't we keep an emphatic notion of truth?

T

Sure, but it's always in the name of *my truth* that I give myself the license to stamp out others' truths...As long as the praxis of truth is bound to that of domination, it remains an anthropomorphic conceit and, as exemplified by historical world events, a violent blinding response of man to mortality. Despite the easy-going character of the statement 'everything goes', nothing is more difficult to assume. People on the spiritual path dedicate their whole lifetime to practising it, but as with everything else, the path is full of thorns, for only when there's nothing at the base, when one has freed oneself of all attachment, does everything truly go. Truth cannot be opposed to 'everything goes', for truth is in between all regimes of truths. It has no name. This is the very challenge it continues to raise with the documentary as technology of truth.

CONTRIBUTORS

Stella Bruzzi is Professor of Film and Television Studies at the University of Warwick. She has researched and taught in several areas, including documentary film and television, costume and film, women's cinema, men's cinema, film aesthetics, film history and theory. She has recently completed the second edition of *New Documentary* (Routledge 2006) and her study of the seminal television documentary series *Seven Up* is to be published in 2007 by the BFI. She is currently working on a study of masculinity and *mise-en-scène* in cinema. Other publications include: *Bringing Up Daddy: Fatherhood and Masculinity in Postwar Hollywood* (BFI 2005); *New Documentary: A Critical Introduction* (Routledge 2000); *Fashion Cultures: Theories, Histories and Analysis* (co-edited, Routledge 2000); *Undressing Cinema: Clothing and Identity in the Movies* (Routledge 1997).

Sergei Dvortsevoy was born in Kazakhstan and worked as an aviation engineer before studying film in Moscow in the early 1990s. His first film which was also his student film, *Chastie* (23 mins), won the Best Short Film in Cinema du Réel (1995), the Grand Prize in Visions de Réel 1995. It was this film and its success in festivals that initially made his reputation and his prize money from the Mercedes Benz Prize in Leipzig enabled him to make *Bread Day* (1998). His films immediately garnered international acclaim, receiving prizes and recognition at festivals around the world, including the nomination of *Bread Day* for the prestigious Joris Ivens Award at the Amsterdam International Documentary Film Festival. The following year his work was presented at the Robert Flaherty Film Seminar, an institution dedicated to Flaherty's adherence to the goal of seeing and depicting the human condition. Dvortsevoy's documentaries are committed to observational film-making. His subjects – people living in and around a Russia in transition – try in their individual ways to eke out an existence, e.g., *In the Dark* (2004). Dvortsevoy proposes: 'observe together with me quietly and everything will happen'.

John Ellis is Professor of Media Arts at Royal Holloway University of London. He is the author of *TV FAQ* (2007), *Seeing Things: Television in the Age of Uncertainty* (2000) and *Visible Fictions* (1982) as well as a contributor to journals such Screen and Media Culture and Society. Between 1982 and 1999 he ran the independent production company Large Door making broadcast TV documentaries on a variety of subjects from world cinema to the food industry. He was a vice-chair of PACT, the independent producers' association, and is now involved in a series of initiatives around the history of TV.

Gareth Evans Gareth Evans is a writer, curator and editor of the international moving image journal *Vertigo* (www.vertigomagazine.co.uk). He contributes regularly to the film pages of *Time Out London* and works as editor and programmer for the *animate!* project (www.animateonline.org). He has devised many festivals (e.g. on Armenia, Romani Cinema, Portugal, JG Ballard and John Berger) and is a programme advisor to the London Film Festival, Encounters Festival Bristol and Norwich International Animation Festival. He is a director of Lux (www.lux.org.uk) and lives in London.

Clarisse Hahn is an artist who lives and works in Paris. Exploring the documentary genre, Hahn creates feature-length documentaries which are presented in cinemas and video installations. The often-extreme subject matter of Hahn's videos is combined with her sustained involvement in the lives of the people she films. She follows her subjects for a minimum of one year; filming, interviewing and becoming part of their daily life. Hahn spent time in the geriatric ward of a hospital, *Hôpital* (1999), followed and shared her flat with a French porn star and her husband, *Ovidie* (2000), and recorded the daily life of Karima, a young Algerian dominatrix, *Karima* (2002). Her most recent film, *Les Protestants* (2005), delves into the complex network of personal and communal values which binds a family together, her own in fact. Hahn's creations come from her desire for intimate communication with her subjects. The video works, combined or juxtaposed in installations, invite the viewer to make transversal readings of the works. (Anne-Sophie Dinant is Hahn's gallerist.)

Eva Hohenberger studied linguistics, communication and media studies in Münster and Osnabrück, Germany. She has a Ph.D. in work on ethnographic film and Jean Rouch (*Die Wirklichkeit des Films. Dokumentarfilm, ethnographischer Film, Jean Rouch.* Hildesheim 1988). Since 1994 she has been a lecturer in media studies at the Ruhr University Bochum. Her special fields of interest are the history, theory and aesthetics of documentary. She edited the books *Bilder des Wirklichen. Texte zur Theorie des Dokumentarfilms* (Berlin 1998) and, together with Judith Keilbach, *Die Gegenwart der Vergangenheit. Dokumentarfilm, Fernsehen und Geschichte* (Berlin 2003). As a former member of FEMINALE, a womens' film festival in Köln, she co-edited Blaue *Wunder. Neue Filme und Videos von Frauen* (Hamburg 1994). At the Feminale she got to know Trinh Minh-ha and published an interview with her in the journal *Frauen und Film* (nr. 60, 1997).

Lina Khatib is a lecturer at the Department of Media Arts, Royal Holloway University of London, where she teaches media theory, world cinema and international television. Her research interests include the relationship between media, identity and politics in the Middle East. She is the author of *Filming the Modern Middle East: Politics in the Cinemas of Hollywood and the Arab World* (2006) and *Lebanese Cinema: Imagining the Civil War and Beyond* (2008). She is the editor of the *Journal of Media Practice* and is a founding co-editor of the *Middle East Journal of Culture and Communication*. She has made two documentary shorts commenting on political culture in the Middle East, *Quelle Révolution* (2006) and *Mapping the South* (2007), with Khaled Ramadan and Stine Hoxbroe.

Gideon Koppel was a postgraduate student at the Slade School of Fine Art working with mixed-media installations and experimental film. His prolific work as a film-maker is exhibited in a wide variety of formats: from the film installation for fashion label Comme des Garcons seen at the Florence Biennale to the acclaimed documentary Channel Four series '*Undressed*'. More recently he made the controversial '*Ooh la la and the art of dressing up*' for BBC Wales which explores the psychopathology of celebrity. Although curiously never broadcast, this film was premiered at the 2004 Sheffield Documentary Festival. Gideon is currently in post-production on his first feature film, executive produced by Mike Figgis and Margaret Matheson. Gideon is a faculty member of Royal Holloway, University of London and teaches with Professor Theodore Zeldin at HEC, Paris.

Cahal McLaughlin is a senior lecturer at the School of Media, Film and Journalism at the University of Ulster. A documentary film-maker with almost twenty years of broadcast and community production experience, he has most recently directed *Inside Stories: Memories of the Maze and Long Kesh Prison* (Catalyst Arts 2005) and *We Never Give Up* (2002) for the Human Rights Media Centre, Cape Town, on Apartheid reparations in South Africa. McLaughlin's writings include contributions to *Keeping It Real: Irish Film and Television* (2004) and *Re-mapping the Field: New Approaches in Conflict Archaeology* (2006). He is director of the Prisons Memory Archive, funded by the Heritage Lottery Fund, of audio-visual recordings from the political prisons in the north of Ireland. He is also the chair of the editorial board of the *Journal of Media Practice*.

Gail Pearce lectures in Contemporary Media Art at Royal Holloway, University of London. Working as an artist in a variety of media, she trained as a sculptor and then worked with film and animation. Recent projects include rediscovering drawing as the source of the digital experience in *Drawn to Love*, in the Digital Love exhibition at the M'Ars Contemporary Art Centre, Moscow. Pearce took part in *emplacements*, a series of international exhibitions, workshops and talks emphasizing place and identity, cultural collaboration and site-specific art in St Petersburg. Three annual video installations culminated in 2003, for the 300th anniversary of the city. Her interactive drama, *Triple Vision*, was broadcast by Videotron's Interactive channel (now Cable & Wireless). She has also made digital and interactive installations, (*Cooking the Books* 2000, *Millennium Fever* 1997, *Mirror, Mirror* 1996). Publications include 'Mirror, Mirror: a context for violence in the home', (ed.) Cutting Edge Research Group, *Desire by Design*, I. B. Tauris, 1999 and 'Drawing on the Digital', *Boiling* animation magazine, Arts Council; 1996.

Nina Pope and Karen Guthrie have collaborated as visual artists for the last decade and in 2001 founded Somewhere – which co-produced *Bata-ville*, their first full-length film. *Bata-ville* (2006) sees Pope & Guthrie reprise their roles as hostesses – first seen in their webcast project */broadcast/* (1999) where they produced a live interpretation of Chaucer's The Canterbury Tales for Tate Modern (London). In *Bata-ville*, they appear in distinctive costume, adopting the roles of travel guides and interpreters for their passengers whilst also pursuing the film's themes with the recurring question 'Are you afraid of the future?' posed to a succession of interviewees which include workers at an airplane factory and cemetery. Pope & Guthrie met in the late 1980s at Edinburgh College of Art, but did not begin their collaboration until 1995 with the multi-media installation *Somewhere Over the TV*. This was followed by one of the Web's earliest artists' projects – the ground-breaking live online travelogue *A Hypertext Journal* in 1996. A succession of commissions for major institutions followed, including Tate Modern, Grizedale Arts and the Institute of Contemporary Arts (where they were awarded the 1999 Imaginaria Digital Art Award). In 2002 Pope & Guthrie produced and curated *TV Swansong*, an innovative live webcast of specially commissioned artists projects. Nina Pope lives and works in London, whilst Karen Guthrie lives in the English Lake District and works both there and in London. Both also maintain solo careers and academic posts at the Royal College of Art (London) and St Martin's College (Lancaster) respectively. They are currently developing new work based on historical re-enactment, as well as a public art commission for Cinema City (Norwich).

Michael Renov is a professor at the University of Southern California's School of Cinematic Arts. His teaching and research interests include documentary theory, autobiography in film and video, video art and activism, and representations of the Holocaust. Professor Renov is the author of *The Subject of Documentary* (2004), editor of *Theorizing Documentary* (1993) and co-editor of *Resolutions: Contemporary Video Practices* (1996) and *Collecting Visible Evidence* (1999). In 1993, while Editor-in-Chief of *Quarterly Review of Film and Video*, Renov co-founded Visible Evidence, a series of international and highly interdisciplinary documentary studies conferences. In 2005, he co-programmed the 51st annual Robert Flaherty Seminar, a week-long gathering of documentary film-makers, curators and educators, creating twenty screening programs and film-maker dialogues on the theme 'Cinema and History'. In addition to curating documentary programmes around the world, he has served as a jury member at documentary festivals including Sundance, Silverdocs and It's All True.

Ann-Sofi Sidén came to the attention of UK audiences with an exhibition at the Hayward Gallery in London, *Warte Mal!* (1999). Using interviews with prostitutes and miscellaneous video material from Dubi, a Czech town close to the German border, the multi-screen exhibition created a 'street' effect, with the videos telling the prostitutes' stories. Sidén's other work includes *QM I think I call her QM* (1997) (co-directed with Tony Gerber), *Who told the chambermaid?* (1999), *Who is invading my privacy, not so quietly and not so friendly?* (2000). The retrospective, *Ann-Sofi Sidén- The Planning Eye Revisited*, was shown at the Musée d'art Moderne de la Ville de Paris in 2001.

Claudia Spinelli is an art critic and curator based in Basel, Switzerland. Since 1994, she has written regularly for the daily press and for art magazines such as Kunst Bulletin, Parkett and Monopol. In collaboration with artist Eric Hattan she curated *Filiale Basel*, 1994–96. As the director of the Kleines Helmhaus, as well as the Kunstverein Galerie Walcheturm (both in Zurich) she curated over 25 exhibitions devoted to young and upcoming artists (e.g. Peter Friedl, Costa Vece, Anna Jermolaewa, Ross Sinclair). Since 2002 she has worked as an independent curator. In collaboration with the international film festival Visions du Réel she has curated the exhibition, *Reprocessing Reality, New Perspectives on Art and the Documentary* (www.reprocessingreality.ch). The first venue was in 2006 at the Chateau de Nyon, followed by P.S.1 Contemporary Art Center in Long Island City, New York (http:///www.ps1.org). Her most recent project is *The Art of Failure*, shown at the Kunsthaus Baselland.

Trinh T. Minh-ha was born in Vietnam and is a film-maker, writer and music composer. Her works include seven films: *Night Passage* (2004, 98 mins) *The Fourth Dimension* (2001, 87 mins), *A Tale of Love* (1995, 108 mins), an experimental narrative, *Shoot for the Contents* (1991, 102 mins), a film on culture, art and politics in China, *Surname Viet Given Name Nam*

(1989, 108 mins), a film on identity and culture through the struggle of Vietnamese women, *Naked Spaces - Living is Round* (1985, 135 mins) and *Reassemblage* (1982, 40 mins); nine books, including *The Digital Film Event* (2005), *Cinema Interval* (1999), *Framer Framed* (1992), *When the Moon Waxes Red* (representation, gender and cultural politics, 1991), *Woman, Native, Other* (post-coloniality and feminism, 1989), *En Minuscules* (poems, 1987), and in collaboration with Jean-Paul Bourdier, *Habiter un Monde* (Paris, 2006), *Drawn from African Dwelling* (1996), *African Spaces - Designs for Living in Upper Volta* (1985); and three large-scale multi-media installations, *Nothing But Ways* (in collaboration with L M Kirby, 1999, Yerba Buena Center for the Arts, San Francisco), *The Desert is Watching* (in collaboration with Jean-Paul Bourdier, 2003, Kyoto Art Biennale) and *L'Autre Marche* (The Other Walk) June 2006 until 2009 at the new Musée du Quai Branly in Paris (France). The recipient of several awards and grants (including the AFI National Independent Filmmaker Maya Deren Award, fellowships from the Guggenheim Foundation, the National Endowment of the Arts, the Rockefeller Foundation, the American Film Institute, The Japan Foundation and the California Arts Council), her films have been given thirty-six retrospectives in the US, the UK, Spain, the Netherlands, Slovenia, France, Germany, Switzerland, Austria, Japan and Hong Kong and were exhibited at the international contemporary art exhibition Documenta 11 (2002) in Germany. Trinh Minh-ha has travelled and lectured extensively — in the States, as well as in Europe, Asia, Australia and New Zealand — on film, art, feminism and cultural politics. She is Professor of Women's Studies and Rhetoric (Film) at the University of California, Berkeley.

Jane and Louise Wilson make video projections, photographs taken during the filming process, and three-dimensional sculptures. Underlying their work is an interest in issues of power, surveillance and paranoia. Their installations explore the psychology and architectural language surrounding certain buildings, as well as investigating sites of political power. Through their documentation of these often bureaucratic buildings, a silent narrative is formed, devoid of human content yet alluding to the ghostly presences of the people who once inhabited them. *Stasi* (1997), a two-screen video installation, was filmed at the headquarters of East German intelligence hastily abandoned with the demise of the Berlin Wall. *Dream Time* (2001) documented the launch of the first manned space mission to the International Space Station from the Russian Baikonur Cosmodrome, and *Broken Time* (2005) is a multi-screen film made of the Great North Run.

BIBLIOGRAPHY

Adams Sitney, P. (1979), *Visionary Film: The American Avant-Garde 1943–1978*. New York: Oxford University Press.

Babbitts, J. (2004), 'Stereographs and the Construction of a Visual Culture in the United States'. In Rabinovitz, L. and Geil, A. (eds.) in *Memory Bytes*. Durham and London: Duke University Press.

Barta, T. (1998), 'Screening the Past: History Since the Cinema'. In Barta, T. (ed.) *Screening the Past: Film and the Representation of History*. London: Praeger.

Barthes, R. (1985), 'On Photography'. In *The Grain of the Voice*. Trans. Coverdale, L. New York: Hill and Wang.

Brakhage, S. (1983), 'The Independent Filmmaker: Stan Brakhage'. In McBride, J., (ed.) *Filmmakers on Filmmaking: The American Film Institute Seminars on Motion Pictures and Television*. Los Angeles: J.P. Tarcher Inc.

Bradley, R. (2003), 'The Translation of Time'. In Van Dyke, R. M. and Alcock, S. E. (eds.) *Archaeologies of Memory*. Oxford: Blackwell.

Bruzzi, S. (2005), *Bringing Up Daddy: Fatherhood and Masculinity in Postwar Hollywood*. London: BFI Publishing.

Bruzzi, S. (2006), *New Documentary* (2nd edition) London: Routledge.

Chamoun, J. (1993), interview with Hassan Bdeir. *Al Ahd* newspaper, 26 November.

Chamoun, J. (2001), interview with George Ki'di. *An-Nahar* newspaper, 13 November.

Clifford J. (1987), 'Of Other Peoples: beyond the "Salvage Paradigm"'. In Foster H. (ed.) *Discussions in Contemporary Culture*. Seattle: Bay Press.

Corner, J. (1996), *The Art of Record; a Critical Introduction to Documentary* Manchester: Manchester University Press.

Deren, M. (1970), 'Poetry and the Film: A Symposium'. In Adams Sitney, P. (ed.) *Film Culture Reader*. New York; Praeger Publishers.

Eitzen, D. (1995), 'When is a Documentary?: Documentary as a Mode of Reception.' *Cinema Journal* 35(1).

Ellis, J. (1982, 1992), *Visible Fictions*. London: Routledge.

Ellis, J. (2000), *Seeing Things: Television in the Age of Uncertainty*. New York: Martin's Press.

Ellis, J. (2005), 'Documentary and Truth on Television: The Crisis of 1999'. In Corner, J. and Rosenthal, A. (eds.) *New Challenges for Documentary* (2nd ed.), Manchester: Manchester University Press.

Ellis, J. (2007), *TV FAQ*. London: I.B. Taurus.

Godmilow, J. (1997), 'How Real is the Reality in Documentary Film?: Interview with Ann-Louise Shapiro'. *History and Theory* 36(4).

Grierson, J. (1966), 'The First Principles of Documentary'. In Hardy, F. (ed.), *Grierson on Documentary*. London: Faber and Faber.

Guynn, W. (1990), *A Cinema of Nonfiction*. London: Associated University Presses.

Harper, S. (1997), 'Popular Film, Popular Memory: The Case of the Second World War'. In Evans, M. and Lunn, K. (eds.) *War and Memory in the Twentieth Century*. Oxford: Berg.

Hohenberger, E. (2006), 'Interview with Trinh T Min Ha'. In Teiss V. and Kull, V. (eds.) *Poeten, Chronisten Rebellen. Internationale DokumentarfilmemacherInnen im Porträt*. Marburg.

Hynes, S. (1999), 'Personal Narratives and Commemoration'. In Winter, J. and Sivan, E. (eds.) *War and Remembrance in the Twentieth Century*. Cambridge: Cambridge University Press.

Ivens, J. (1969), *The Camera and I*. New York: International Publishers.

Jones, S. (1998), 'Marcel Ophüls' *November Days*: The Forming and Performing of Documentary History'. In Barta, T. (ed.), *Screening the Past: Film and the Representation of History*. London: Praeger.

Joyce, R. A. (2003), 'Concrete Memories: Fragments of the Classic Maya Past (500–1000AD)'. In Van Dyke, R. M. and Alcock, S. E. (eds.) *Archaeologies of Memory*. Oxford: Blackwell.

Lesage, J. (1999), 'Women's Fragmented Consciousness'. In *Feminism and Documentary*. Waldman, D. and Walker, J. *Visible Evidence 5*. Minneapolis: University of Minnesota Press.

Mamber, S. (1974), *Cinema Verite in America: Studies in Uncontrolled Documentary*. Cambridge: MIT Press.

McLaughlin, C. (2004), 'Telling Our Story: The Springhill Massacre'. In Barton, R. and O'Brien, H. (eds.) *Keeping It Real: Irish Film and Television*. London: Wallflower Press.

McLaughlin, C. (2006), 'Touchstone and Tinderbox: documenting memories inside the north of Ireland's Long Kesh and Maze Prison'. In Schofield, J. et al. (eds.) *Re-mapping the Field: New Approaches in Conflict Archaeology*. Berlin: Westkreuz-Verlag.

Merridale, C. (1999), 'War, Death, and Remembrance in Soviet Russia'. In Winter, J. and Sivan, E. (eds.) *War and Remembrance in the Twentieth Century*. Cambridge: Cambridge University Press.

Michelson, A. (ed.) (1984), *Kino-Eye: The Writings of Dziga Vertov*. Berkeley: University of California Press.

Moran, J. M. (1999), 'A Bone of Contention: Documenting the Prehistoric Subject'. In Gaines, J. M. and Renov, M. (eds.) *Collecting Visible Evidence*. Minneapolis: University of Minnesota Press.

Nichols, B. (1987), 'History, Myth and Narrative in Documentary'. *Film Quarterly* 41(1).

Nichols, B. (1991), *Representing Reality: Issues and Concepts in Documentary*. Bloomington: Indiana University Press.

Nichols, B. (1994), *Blurred Boundaries*. Bloomington: Indiana University Press.

Nichols, B. (2001), *Introduction to Documentary*. Bloomington: Indiana University Press.

Pearce, G. (1999), 'Mirror, Mirror: a context for violence in the home', in Cutting Edge Research Group, (eds.) *Desire by Design*. London: I B Tauris.

Pearce, G. (1996), 'Drawing on the Digital'. *Boiling* 1(1). London: Arts Council.

Peillex, G. (1964), *Nineteenth Century Painting*. London: Weidenfeld and Nicolson.

Rabinowitz, P. (1993), 'Wreckage upon Wreckage: History, Documentary and the Ruins of Memory'. *History and Theory* 32(2).

Renov, M. (1993), 'Toward a Poetics of Documentary'. In Renov, M. (ed.) *Theorizing Documentary*, New York: Routledge.

Russell C. (1999), *Experimental Ethnography The Work of Film in the Age of Video*. Durham and London: Duke University Press.

Samuel, R. (1994), *Theatres of Memory*. London: Verso.

Shaw, Martin (1997), 'Past Wars and Present Conflicts: From the Second World War to the Gulf War'. In Evans, M. and Lunn, K. (eds.) *War and Memory in the Twentieth Century*. Oxford: Berg.

Sherman S. R. (1998), *Documenting Ourselves; Film, Video and Culture*. Lexington: University Press of Kentucky.

Sklar, R. (1975), 'Documentary: Artifice in the Service of Truth'. *Reviews in American History* 3(3).

Sorlin, P. (1999), 'Children as War Victims in Postwar European Cinema'. In Winter, J. and Sivan, E. (eds.) *War and Remembrance in the Twentieth Century*. Cambridge: Cambridge University Press.

Stott, W. (1973), *Documentary Expression and Thirties America*. Oxford: Oxford University Press.

Tobing Rony, F. (1996), *The Third Eye: Race, Cinema and Ethnographic Spectacle*. Durham, N.C.: Duke University Press.

Trinh, T. M. (1990), 'Documentary Is/Not a Name'. *October 52*.

Tyler, S. A. (1986), 'Post-Modern Ethnography'. In Clifford, J. and Marcus, G. E. (eds.) *Writing Culture: The Poetics and Politics of Ethnography*. Berkeley: University of California Press.

Van Dyke, R. M. and Alcock, S. E. (2003), 'Archaeologies of Memory: An Introduction'. In Van Dyke, R. M. and Alcock, S. E. (eds.), *Archaeologies of Memory*. Oxford: Blackwell.

Williams, L. (1993), 'Mirrors without Memories: Truth, History and the New Documentary'. *Film Quarterly*, 46 (3).

Winston, B. (1995), *Claiming the Real: The Griersonian Documentary and Its Legitimations*. London: British Film Institute.

Winter, J. and Sivan, E. (1999), Setting the Framework. In Winter, J. and Sivan, E. (eds.), *War and Remembrance in the Twentieth Century*. Cambridge: Cambridge University Press.

Wollen, P. (1969), *Signs and Meaning in the Cinema*. Bloomington: Indiana University Press.

INDEX